Shhh!

Oranges
and
Peaches

LEGO minifigures

CHARACTER ENCYCLOPEDIA

FEATURING MORE THAN 160 MINIFIGURES

WRITTEN BY DANIEL LIPKOWITZ

Contents

Meet The Minifigures

THE COLLECTIBLE MINIFIGURES truly are the stars of this book, with a separate page on each and every one. Filled with fascinating facts, the Minifigure profiles tell you everything you need to know about all the quirky and colorful characters. The book is divided into ten chapters—one chapter for each of the ten random collectible Minifigures series. The collectible Minifigures have a capital "M", whereas any LEGO® minifigures from other themes are in lower-case. Told you the collectibles are the stars!

THERE IS A PARTY ON ONE OF THESE PAGES AND I'M OFF TO FIND IT!

PARRRTAY!

HEH HEH HEH!

How a **Minifigure** is **Made**

HOW DOES THE LEGO® MINIFIGURES design team create a new Minifigure? With more than 160 characters in the growing lineup so far, it may sound difficult to keep coming up with new personalities, accessories, and designs, but these creative builders make it look easy. Here's how it's done!

Minifigure design team

Gitte
Senior Element Sculptor

Niels
Element Sculptor

Laurence
Design Manager

Matthew
Vice President

Ashley
Element Designer

Tara
Design Manager

Chris
Senior Graphic Designer

Stewart
Element Sculptor

1 Brainstorming

The process begins more than a year before the new series of Minifigures is released. The design team creates a list of possible characters after holding brainstorming meetings and looking at fan requests. Everybody wants to come up with the next great Minifigure idea!

> I TAUGHT THESE GUYS EVERYTHING THEY KNOW!

LEGO Offices, Billund

Sketches

The team sits down with sketches of their favorite ideas. The designers then shuffle ideas around to come up with 16 very different characters. They consider the time of year when the series will be released, what designs would go well with current LEGO® themes, characters that complement ones from earlier LEGO Minifigures series, and figures that they personally want to make! The designers especially like to create characters that might not get made outside of the LEGO Minifigures line, as well as ones that can inspire new LEGO building ideas.

2

Early sketches and computer-aided designs.

3

Designing

Now it's time for the designers to start designing! They figure out what new elements will be needed and either sculpt them out of clay at a 3-to-1 scale or create them digitally on a computer. They decide on the colors and printed decoration that each character will have, and research to make sure that they include all of the important details. A LEGO graphic designer works from sketches and other image references to create the printed details for each character.

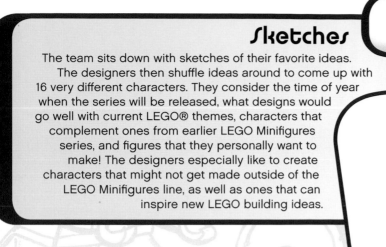

3D Rendering

4

Once the designs are complete, computer models are created with signature poses for each character. These will be featured on the bags and boxes in which the Minifigures are finally packaged in. A writer then creates biographies to give each Minifigure its own fun and unique personality. The LEGO.com web team makes online pages, games, and smart-phone applications that feature the new characters. Finally, about a month before they're released, the latest series of 16 LEGO Minifigures is revealed to the public…and then it's time to start all over again!

Series 1

MAY 2010 The first series of the LEGO®
Minifigures set the pattern for the
brand-new toy line. The series comprises
16 quirky and original new characters.
They came in unmarked bags,
so you couldn't discover which
Minifigure you were going to
get until you opened the pack.

A CURIOUS PLANET,
THEY ALL SEEM
TO LIKE WAVING!

Super
Wrestler

Demolition
Dummy

Cowboy

Nurse

Robot

Tribal
Hunter

Spaceman

Cheerleader

A friend who is there to cheer you on

THE PERKY, peppy Cheerleader is a constant source of inspiration to the other Minifigures. She always has something positive to say to encourage people, whether they are playing an important game or just changing a lightbulb. Anyone who watches one of her enthusiastic cheer routines finds her unshakeable good mood totally contagious.

The first appearance of this hair piece in blonde

Did You Know?

The "M" on the Cheerleader's top stands for the first initial of the Vice President of the LEGO Group Matthew Ashton.

Hands fit inside the pom-poms

Cheerful Disposition

The Cheerleader doesn't care what team you are on. As long as you try your best and don't give up, she will be on your side!

The Cheerleader prefers handsprings and cartwheels to plain-old walking

Rare printing on the side of the legs

Mini Facts

Likes: Smiles and sunny days

Dislikes: Nothing

See Also: Football Player (S8), Red Cheerleader (S8)

Circus Clown

A fun-loving fellow for whom everything's a joke

WHENEVER THINGS get dull or gloomy, you can count on the Circus Clown to make you laugh. Life is all fun and games to this colorful character. Just don't expect to have a deep conversation, because he communicates by simply honking his horn.

This is the first use of this new hair element

Mini Facts

Likes: Laughter

Dislikes: When things get serious

See Also: Ringmaster (S2), Small Clown (S5), Sad Clown (S10)

At The Circus

Many of the Minifigures are designed to be part of a running theme. Put the Circus Clown with the Small Clown, and the Ringmaster and you have got your very own miniature circus troupe!

Did You Know?

There are just four types of LEGO® musical instrument accessories in the Minifigures range.

The Circus Clown is currently the only character that features this horn

Different colored plastic used for each leg and painted patches create a goofy pair of pants

THESE TWO HAVE REALLY PUT ME IN A GOOD MOOD. NOW, WHERE IS THAT PARTY...?

Super Wrestler

A masked Minifigure with the moves to win

THE THREE THINGS most important to the Super Wrestler are his honor, his mask, and wrestling. He treats every challenge he encounters like his latest match, relying on his strength and sense of justice to win the day. You may not think you can solve all of life's problems with flashy wrestling moves, but somehow it works.

Mask has holes for his eyes and mouth

ARE YOU READY TO FIGHT?!

...

Wrestling Mania

The Super Wrestler has yet to find another masked wrestler to fight. Fortunately, there are plenty of other challengers willing to test their might against his in the ring.

Fabric cape for a grand entrance into the wrestling ring

Printed muscles to show his strength

World championship belt

Did You Know?

The Super Wrestler's masked face is printed on a rare blue LEGO Minifigure head.

Mini Facts

Likes: Wrestling

Dislikes: Losing his mask

See Also: Sumo Wrestler (S3), Boxer (S5)

Tribal Hunter

An expert at tracking down lost objects

THE TRIBAL HUNTER is the best person to help locate lost items. No matter what you have misplaced, he will hunt it down. He is so good at finding things, no one will play hide-and-seek with him! He is also a great dancer, but very shy. When he goes to a dance party, he always wears a disguise.

Accessorizing

Minifigures can carry accessories in several ways. Some clip into their hands, some go on their heads, and others (like backpacks and arrow-quivers) go over their neck posts and are held in place by their head.

Mini Facts

Likes: Dance tunes

Dislikes: Being seen dancing

See Also: Tribal Chief (S3), Flamenco Dancer (S6)

Feathers attach to the back of the hair piece

Bead and feather necklace

Fringed buckskin tracking outfit

Did You Know?

The Tribal Hunter's accessories originated from the 1996 LEGO Western theme.

11

Skater

A speed demon who can't bear to be second best

NO ONE IS MORE competitive than the Skater, and if someone says they are, he will race them for the title. His skateboard is his prized possession; he will keep it clean and shiny even if he gets in a total mess himself. He practices all the time to be the fastest thing on wheels, and while he hasn't succeeded yet, he is definitely getting there.

THINK YOU'RE FASTER THAN ME? LET'S FIND OUT!

Speed Skater

If something moves quickly, the Skater will race against it. He can't stand to see anything faster than him!

Hair piece originally appeared in brown on the LEGO® Club mascot minifigure, Max

Radical skull hoodie sweatshirt

Mini Facts

Likes: Being the fastest

Dislikes: Losing a race

See Also: Street Skater (S4), Skater Girl (S6)

Did You Know?

When the LEGO Minifigures were tested with kids before their release, the Skater was a clear favorite. His popularity won him a starring spot in the first series.

Skateboard wheels really spin

LEGO studs on the skateboard hold the feet in place

Deep Sea Diver

A water lover who is a little hard to understand

THE DEEP SEA DIVER is full of exciting stories about his adventures under the sea. Unfortunately, nobody knows what they are because the only sounds that can be heard through his diving mask and air tank are blubs and burbles. He can often be found swimming around in bathtubs looking for exotic fish.

Diving mask can flip up and down

Wetsuit keeps out the cold at extreme underwater depths

Mini Facts

Likes: Walking in flippers

Dislikes: Tripping

See Also: Surfer (S2), Diver (S8)

IS THAT REALLY WHAT YOU WEAR FOR YOUR MORNING RUN?

Flippers On Land

Why does the Deep Sea Diver never take off his gear? He has spent so much time underwater that he's forgotten you can breathe on land!

Did You Know?

This was the first time the classic LEGO diving tank accessory was produced in orange.

Flippers connect to the soles of his feet

13

Cowboy

A rootin', tootin' hero of the Old West

THE COWBOY loves to show off his pistols. He is a master of the lucky shot and can hit just about any target from any distance. He is also impeccably honest and a true gentleman—he always raises his hat to anyone he meets. These skills have helped him get out of a lot of sticky situations.

Removable cowboy hat

A hard-working cowpoke doesn't always have time to shave

Mini Facts

Likes: Camping

Dislikes: Bad manners

See Also: Bandit (S6), Cowgirl (S8)

Bandolier filled with spare bullets

Large silver belt buckle in true Texas style

MY HORSE MUST BE HERE SOMEWHERE!

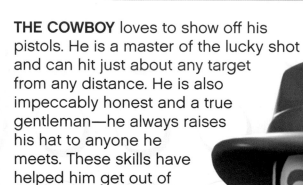

Horseless Hero

The Cowboy never stays in one town for long—he's always out on the trail trying to find his lost horse.

MAYBE THE DEEP SEA DIVER HAS A SEAHORSE HE CAN LEND YA, PARDNER! HAW HAW!

14

Nurse

A friendly professional who is here to help

THE NURSE is devoted to making everybody around her feel better, no matter what she has to put them through to do it. She will wrap a patient in bandages from head to toe to treat a bruised knee, or build a fully functional MRI scanner for a sprained elbow. As long as the problem is eventually fixed, she knows she has done her job!

DON'T WORRY! I CAN CURE YOU.

First Aid

The well-meaning Nurse believes that everything can be cured with proper medical care—whether you are feeling physically sick or not!

New syringe element was later used as a tranquilizer dart in the LEGO Dino series

The Nurse was the first Minifigure to have this hair piece

Mini Facts

Likes: Curing patients

Dislikes: The common cold

See Also: Skier (S2), Surgeon (S6)

Star of Life symbol used by emergency medical workers around the world

Did You Know?

LEGO Minifigures designer Laurence Dawes is the patient named on the Nurse's chart.

Magician

A stylish showman who likes to play tricks

THE MAGICIAN loves to put on a spectacle and display baffling magical feats to his audience. With a wave of his wand, he can pull any object you can name out of his hat. But he is also a big prankster, so don't forget to check your pockets after the show—the handkerchief he conjured up might just be your own.

Alternate Appearance

Some Minifigures include extra parts so you can change the way they look. The Magician comes with a separate hair piece, that can be used when he isn't wearing his top hat.

Elegantly waxed moustache

Slightly mischievous expression

Mini Facts

Likes: Appreciative audiences

Dislikes: Uncooperative rabbits

See Also: Bunny Suit Guy (S7), Fortune Teller (S9)

Did You Know?

LEGO bar elements aren't usually painted, but the Magician's wand was given special treatment.

Magic wand is three quarters of the length of a traditional LEGO bar

Professional magician's tuxedo

Demolition Dummy

An odd individual who is totally into deconstruction

ALL THE DEMOLITION DUMMY knows how to do is to take things apart. He disassembles everything he comes across, leaving piles of bricks behind him wherever he goes. He does not do it to be mean—it's just his nature. At least after he visits, you have the opportunity to build something new.

Mini Facts

Likes: Brick walls

Dislikes: One-piece objects

See Also: Robot (S1)

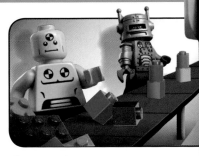

Opposites In Action

The Robot constantly builds, and the Demolition Dummy constantly takes things apart. Put them in the same room and they act like a perpetual motion machine!

No one knows what the Demolition Dummy is actually thinking

Did You Know?

The "PA7 70" on the license plate is a reference to LEGO designer Michael Patton.

Wrench for taking bricks apart

Crash-test markings

Based on the crash-test dummies used to improve automobile safety

License plate from a dismantled car

PA7 70

17

Forestman

A gallant archer who excels at feats of bravery

THE SWASHBUCKLING Forestman lives to rescue maidens, battle evil dukes, and bring food to hungry peasants. Most of all, he likes to make a really memorable entrance, whether he is scaling castle battlements or swinging through on ropes. After all, when you are saving the day, it is important to make a good first impression.

Removable feather plume

Did You Know?

The Forestman is an homage to a certain legendary outlaw from English folklore.

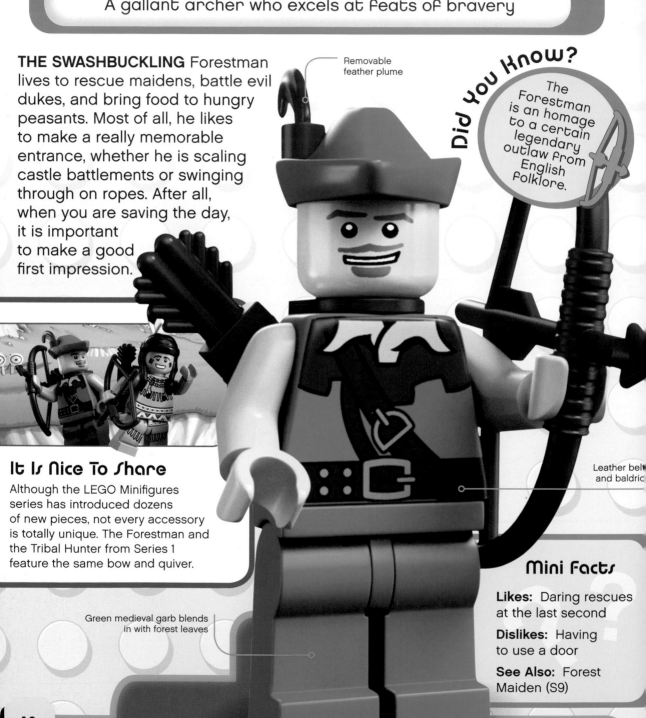

It Is Nice To Share

Although the LEGO Minifigures series has introduced dozens of new pieces, not every accessory is totally unique. The Forestman and the Tribal Hunter from Series 1 feature the same bow and quiver.

Green medieval garb blends in with forest leaves

Leather belt and baldric

Mini Facts

Likes: Daring rescues at the last second

Dislikes: Having to use a door

See Also: Forest Maiden (S9)

Ninja

A master of stealth he isn't

ALTHOUGH HE HAS TRAINED for years to be a silent warrior of the night, the Ninja just hasn't been able to grasp the whole "sneaky" aspect of the job. It is not that he doesn't know how to fade into the shadows, but his natural clumsiness makes him fall back out of them again. Plus, he is afraid of the dark.

The Ninja's ancient and mystical katana blade is used mostly for making sandwiches

Did You Know?

The Ninja is another character with a connection to a classic LEGO® Castle series: the Ninja sub-theme from 1998.

Removable mask has a clip for storing his sword on the back

Mini Facts

Likes: Being a ninja

Dislikes: Not being a good one

See Also: Samurai Warrior (S3)

Origin Of A Ninja

The Ninja's unmasked face shows his determination to someday become a true master of Ninjutsu. As a baby, he was found on the doorstep of his clan's temple with a note that read, "Please make me a ninja!"

Black ninja garb blends into shadows… in theory

KEEP PRACTICING! I ALMOST DIDN'T SPOT YOU THIS TIME!

19

Caveman

An inventor who is ahead of his time

THE CREATIVE

Caveman is constantly coming up with new inventions, but someone else has always thought of them first: fire, the wheel, and even a primitive rock-based construction brick... he has been beaten to the punch on every one. It is a good thing nobody has invented crankiness yet, or he might really get mad!

Did You Know?

The Caveman is the only character in the LEGO Minifigures line with a unibrow.

The Caveman was the first Minifigure to carry this new spiked stone club

A tattered hide is the very height of prehistoric fashion

When buttons haven't been invented yet, try a bone instead

Hidden Features

The LEGO designers like to give Minifigure characters fully painted faces even when they are mostly hidden by helmets or facial hair. Removing a beard can sometimes reveal an unexpected expression.

Mini Facts

Likes: Inventing new objects

Dislikes: Not inventing them first

See Also: Cave Woman (S5)

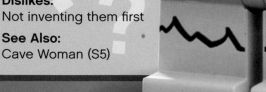

Spaceman

A cosmic explorer who is out of this world

THE SPACEMAN is a little bit confused. Even when he's home on planet Earth, he acts like he is still out exploring the cosmos. Not only does he walk in giant bounding leaps, but he thinks that every Minifigure he meets is a strange new alien species. Of course, he is right some of the time.

Removable space helmet with detachable visor

The Intrepid Astronaut

The Spaceman sets out each day eager to explore his new territory. He's actually been on Earth a very long time, but he still steps outside like he is forging a new frontier.

Mini Facts

Likes: Friendly alien encounters

Dislikes: Hostile alien attacks

See Also:
Space Alien (S3),
Space Villain (S3),
Intergalactic Girl (S6)

Symbol of the classic LEGO® Space theme from 1978

Electro-Zapp blaster was later used in the LEGO® Alien Conquest theme

Clear blue short bar element becomes a laser beam

Magnetic boots for walking on walls and ceilings in low gravity

Did You Know?

Created by Lawrence Dawes, the Spaceman's new laser gun was an immediate favorite among the LEGO designers.

21

Robot

A mechanical marvel programed for building

THE CLANKING, beeping Robot tirelessly searches the world for spare bricks. When he finds them, he stacks them into incredibly huge structures, not stopping until he has used every piece. He works so hard that sometimes he forgets to recharge his circuits and freezes up mid-build.

Retro look styled after the clunky robots of low-budget 1950s sci-fi movies

Metallic silver paint

Gauge measures whether enough bricks have been found to start building

Powerful pneumatic claw assembles bricks at ten times the normal speed

Bolts provide easy access to internal components for maintenance

Beneath The Bucket

Under his helmet (which was first created for this character), the Robot has a detailed face, with photo-receptor eyes and a mouth-like speaker grille.

Mini Facts

Likes: Building

Dislikes: Rusting

See Also: Clockwork Robot (S6), Evil Robot (S8)

BZZT! WHAT-EV-ER YOU BUILD, I WILL DE-STROY!

Zombie

A thoroughly misunderstood monster

EVERYTHING THE ZOMBIE does is slow, mindless and repetitive. When he tries to accomplish a task, he will keep trying to do it no matter what happens to be in his way, which can lead him to bump into walls and other obstacles over and over again. Fortunately, he doesn't seem to feel a thing.

Red eyes from too many late nights digging and filling in holes

Mini Facts

Likes: His turkey leg

Dislikes: Deep thoughts

See Also: Mummy (S3), The Monster (S4)

The Zombie's updated turkey leg piece has a longer handle than earlier versions

SO...WHAT ARE WE STANDING IN LINE FOR?

Nothing Spooky Here

The Zombie may look a little scary, but he's really quite harmless. All he wants to do is watch TV, wait in lines, and build long, boring brick walls that are all exactly the same size and shape.

The Zombie rarely has a chance to visit a tailor

Series 2

SEPTEMBER 2010 More monsters, more historical figures, and more zany characters! Where else but in series two could you find a leisure-suited disco dancer, a maraca-wielding musician, a bold Spartan warrior, and a multi-faced mime artist all in one place?

ERM, WHERE ARE ALL THE PYRAMIDS?

Pharaoh

Explorer

Pop Star

Ringmaster

Surfer

Weightlifter

Vampire

Maraca Man

CAN ANYONE DO THE SHUFFLE?
....
Traffic Cop
Disco Dude
Mime
Witch
Brick Fever
211
Karate Master
Spartan Warrior
Lifeguard
Skier

Pharaoh

An ancient king stuck in the modern age

EVER SINCE he woke up in the museum, the Pharaoh has been feeling a little out of sorts due to all of the noise and technology of the modern world. Thanks to the Robot, who is helping him build a few pyramids, things are finally starting to feel a bit more like home.

Mini Facts

Likes: Pyramids, chariots, deserts

Dislikes: Skyscrapers, cars, malls

See Also: Mummy (S3), Egyptian Queen (S5)

Staff for waving around and telling people to build faster

Did You Know?

The Pharaoh's cobra-headed staff was designed especially for him.

Golden headdress has a LEGO stud on the forehead for decorations

Royal eyeliner

Linen skirt keeps the Pharaoh cool on hot days in the desert

In The Old Days

Another running theme of the LEGO® Minifigures series is characters from classic historical periods. Whether their adventures take place in the distant past or today is up to whoever is playing with them.

Explorer

A globe-trotting traveler looking for something new

THE EXPLORER has dedicated his life to searching for new and exciting discoveries. Some of those finds (such as particularly interesting-looking pebbles) are mostly only exciting to him, but he doesn't let that stop him from crisscrossing the globe and writing down everything he sees in his exploration journal.

Pith helmet for protection in rockslides or cave-ins

YOU WON'T FIND ANY SEA MONSTERS HERE.

ARE YOU QUITE SURE?

By Jove!

Despite all of his experience traveling around the world, the Explorer has a terrible sense of direction. He sometimes gets lost in his own backyard.

Binoculars for long-distance viewing

Monocle for looking extra-classy at dinner parties

Magnifying glass for up-close examination

Mini Facts

Likes: Things he hasn't seen before

Dislikes: Maps

See Also: Pilot (S3)

Did You Know?

The transparent lens of the Explorer's magnifying glass really works!

MAYBE AN EXPLORER CAN HELP ME FIND THE PARTY!

27

Surfer

A radical dude who is totally bodacious

THE SURFER spends all of his time hanging ten and relaxing in the surf and sand. You can find him on beaches all around the world, up on his board wherever the sun is shining and the waves are wild. The only trick is figuring out what he is saying through all of his surfer-talk!

Did You Know!

The Surfer includes the first-ever printed LEGO surfboard.

Hair bleached by the sun

Decorative Details

Specially decorated accessories help the Minifigures characters really stand out from each other. The Surfer's board is covered with a tropical-island motif that fits his laid-back personality.

Surfing is an excellent way to keep in shape

Mini Facts

Likes: Bodacious waves

Dislikes: The winter

See Also: Lifeguard (S2), Surfer Girl (S4)

Swimming trunks match board detail

28

Surfboard can connect to other LEGO pieces

Lifeguard

A beach patroller who swims to the rescue

SWIMMERS KNOW they are safe when the watchful Lifeguard is around. From her tall chair, she can see everything that happens on the beach. If she spots any trouble, she is off in a flash, in the water with a splash, and on her way. And she always waits half an hour after eating before going on duty.

Hair piece is shared with the Cheerleader

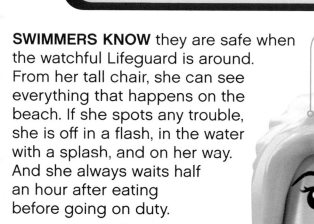

I HAVE SO MUCH STUDYING TO DO...

HEY! I'M NOT WAVING YOU KNOW?

Mini Facts

Likes: Following the safety rules

Dislikes: Splashing in the pool

See Also: Swimming Champion (S7)

Off-The-Clock Training

The Lifeguard has such a passion for learning life-saving techniques that she's started studying at medical school in her spare time.

Rescue can has extra grips for towing tired swimmers

Life preserver logo on swimsuit

Did You Know?

If you look closely, you can see the initials of LEGO sculptor Gitte Thorsen printed on the Lifeguard's swimsuit.

YOU CALL THAT A SWIMSUIT?!

G.T

Traffic Cop

A by-the-book policeman who upholds the law

THE TRAFFIC COP cares a lot about safety. After all, it is his job to enforce it by making sure the other Minifigures always follow the traffic rules. Break the law in his city and you might just find yourself with a speeding ticket, or hauled off in his trusty set of handcuffs.

Helmet for high-speed pursuits

Small Print

The tiny text on the Traffic Cop's printed ticket tile identifies him as a member of the Highway Patrol. He takes his job pretty seriously; he once pulled over a flying saucer for flying over the speed limit!

Highway patrolman's badge

Police radio for talking to HQ

Did you Know?

LEGO Minifigures designer Tara Wike's signature appears on the Traffic Cop's ticket.

Handcuffs can be placed on other minifigures

Mini Facts

Likes: Law-abiding drivers

Dislikes: Speeders

See Also: Race Car Driver (S3), Policeman (S9)

Mime

A silent performer of many moods

DO YOU HEAR somebody being silly behind you? If not, then the Mime is probably back there putting on a show for the passers-by. With his talent for imitation and pantomime, he is second only to the Circus Clown in getting people to laugh—but unlike his horn-honking pal, he does it without making a single sound.

Mini Facts

Likes: Invisible boxes

Dislikes: Squeaky shoes

See Also: Circus Clown (S1), Librarian (S10)

All-new beret element

Extra heads for more expressions

SO YOU WANT TO HEAR ANOTHER SONG, DO YOU?

....

Face The Music

Being silent can mean you make the most unlikely friends. The Popstar often mistakes the Mime's silence for an eagerness to listen to a full rendition of her new album.

Arms painted to show striped sleeves

Did You Know?

The Mime is the first minifigure to be made entirely in black and white.

Vampire

A frightfully friendly creature of the night

AFTER TWO CENTURIES of un-life, the Vampire has become a little bored with the more traditional activities of his kind. These days, he is happy to hang around his castle reading comic books and drinking fruit smoothies. He also likes nighttime strolls on the beach and throwing lavish parties.

Faithful bat friend is trained to fetch the newspaper

Toothy winning smile

LET'S PARRRTAY!

A DROP C THE FINES JUICE, SIP

Well-Dressed Monster

The Vampire likes nothing more than a festive gathering with a good selection of fruit juice. He and the waiter often work together to host the best parties.

Did You Know?

The Vampire has shared his hair piece (in other colors) with Count Dooku from LEGO® *Star Wars*™ and The Joker from Batman™.

The Vampire always wears his finest clothes in case someone drops by

Mini Facts

Likes: Visitors

Dislikes: Door-to-door salesmen

See Also: Werewolf (S4), Vampire Bat (S8)

32

Witch

A sorceress whose spells are slightly askew

THE WITCH wants to be good, but she finds it hard to control her magic powers. Even when she tries to be nice, the result is just a little bit wicked. For example, she turned a neighbor's vegetables into a candy garden for the local kids and accidentally gave the whole town stomach aches!

Broom for riding (and cleaning up miscast magic)

Healthy green skin tone

Mini Facts

Likes: Halloween

Dislikes: Enchanted frogs

See Also: Fairy (S8), Mr. Good and Evil (S9)

A Menagerie Of Monsters

Watch out! The LEGO Minifigures line is full of monsters! Fortunately, most of them are pretty friendly, and they don't usually bite.

Printed potion vial and book of spells

A sloped brick on the lower body creates a witch's robe

Did You Know?

The Witch is the only character in the LEGO Minifigures line whose head is this shade of green. She is also the first to use a LEGO® slope base instead of legs.

At The Beach

IT IS A WARM DAY and the beach is full of Minifigures who have come out for some fun in the sun, sea, and sand. Some want to show off their tan, while others are diving for sunken treasure. This really is the hottest spot in town.

Spartan Warrior

A solider looking for the next big battle

New spear
with a soft
plastic point

THE SPARTAN WARRIOR loves to fight more than anything else in the world, and he exercises and trains to make sure he is always in peak condition for combat. Unfortunately for him (but fortunately for everybody else), things are pretty peaceful right now, so he mostly sits around on the couch watching historical documentaries.

Did You Know?

The Spartan Warrior is a fan-favorite minifigure. At least one LEGO fan has collected 300 of him!

Bearded Brawler

With his gritted teeth and a squinting eye, the Spartan Warrior is ready for action.... or maybe he's just eager for the commercial break to end.

Mini Facts

Likes: Fighting

Dislikes: Not fighting

See Also: Viking (S4), Gladiator (S5), Roman Soldier (S6)

Round shield has a handle on the back and a building stud in front

Legs with printed battle skirt and sandals

HE LOOKS TOUGH! I HOPE TOY SOLDIERS DON'T HAVE TO DO MUCH FIGHTING.

Skier

An accident-prone optimist who won't give up

EVERY TIME THE SKIER goes skiing, he ends up plunging off a cliff, crashing into a tree, or flying through the air. But despite his terrible luck, he takes on every downhill challenge that comes his way. After all, there is always a chance he may stay on his skis the next time.

Mini Facts

Likes: Tricky slopes

Dislikes: Unexpected snow banks

See Also: Nurse (S1), Snowboarder (S3), Downhill Skier (S8)

Cold Competition
Even the Skater can beat the clumsy Skier to the bottom of a snowy slope.

Snug ski cap keeps ears warm during tumbles on the snow

Did You Know?
The Skier can hold both of his skis (placed bottom to bottom) in one hand, and both of his ski poles (clipped together by their notches) in the other.

Tinted lenses to block the sun's glare off the snow

Crossed ski symbol above racing number

Skis can attach to feet

211

37

Karate Master

A skilled fighter who just keeps on training

THE KARATE MASTER has studied many forms of martial arts, but karate is his favorite. Although he has earned a black belt, he continues to practice and perfect his skills, and he loves to teach them to others. He is always willing to demonstrate how he can chop things in half with his bare hands.

Mini Facts

Likes: Chopping demonstrations

Dislikes: Sore hands

See Also: Ninja (S1), Sumo Wrestler (S3)

AND FOR THE NEXT THING THAT I'LL CHOP...

BUT THAT'S MY FAVORITE PARCHMENT TILE!

Symbol of the Karate Master's training center

Traditional martial arts uniform

Black belt, the highest rank

First Prize

His gold trophy is just one of the many awards that the Karate Master has earned in competitions all around the world.

Did You Know?

The Karate Master's mini-statue element is the smallest official scaled representation of a LEGO minifigure.

Maraca Man

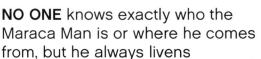

A man of mystery who likes to shake things up

NO ONE knows exactly who the Maraca Man is or where he comes from, but he always livens things up when he is around. With a shake of his rattling maracas, he can turn any gathering into a party. Once everyone is clapping their hands and tapping their feet, he goes on to his next destination.

New sombrero hat piece

Poncho to keep off the dust, wind, and rain on his travels

Brightly colored maracas

Patterned Poncho

The Maraca Man's poncho is a variation of the classic minifigure cape. It is made out of two identical fabric pieces, one in front and one at the back.

Did You Know?

The intricate printing on the sombrero and maracas, and the new textile pattern on his poncho, were a complex challenge for the LEGO designers.

Mini Facts

Likes: Rattling maracas

Dislikes: Rattling rattlesnakes

See Also: Hula Dancer (S3)

Ringmaster

A presenter who loves being in the spotlight

THE RINGMASTER is in charge of the whole circus. He is responsible for making sure the trained animals are well fed, the tightropes are properly secured, and the clowns don't run out of pies to throw. It is a lot to do, but it is all worth it when the audience at the ringside starts to clap and cheer.

The Ringmaster has the same hat-maker and moustache-waxer as the Magician

Lion tamer's whip—this is the only time this element has appeared in white

Mini Facts

Likes: Applause

Dislikes: Peanut shells

See Also: Circus Clown (S1), Small Clown (S5)

Animal Act

The Ringmaster is happy to have a pair of hilarious clowns in his circus troupe, but he really wishes there were more animals in the LEGO Minifigures line.

Smart red jacket is kept spotlessly clean

Did You Know?

Although the LEGO top hat has been in production for more than 15 years, this is its first use on an official Ringmaster minifigure.

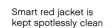

Weightlifter

A strongman who never stops testing his limits

THE WEIGHTLIFTER has sworn to become the strongest LEGO Minifigure in the world. If an object looks bigger and heavier than the last thing he lifted, then he'll try to pick it up and raise it above his head. He started out with pebbles and twigs, but these days he is bench-pressing trucks and houses.

Sweat drop from strenuous exertion

Assembly Required

Some Minifigure accessories are made out of multiple pieces. The Weightlifter's barbell is built with two weight pieces on the ends and a short bar as a handle in between.

Mini Facts

Likes: Lifting things

Dislikes: Dropping things on his toes

See Also: Sumo Wrestler (S3), Fitness Instructor (S5)

Lifting belt protects lower back when hoisting heavy loads

Did you know?

The new weights were designed with standard LEGO brick connections so they could also be used when building models.

Weightlifting uniform with LEGO brick and barbell logos

Disco Dude

A dance machine who is stuck in the 1970s

THE DISCO DUDE loves the 1970s—the era when disco music, bell-bottom pants, and the first LEGO® Space and Castle sets were popular. Whenever he hears disco music playing he heads to the nearest dance floor to show off his moves under a spinning disco ball.

The Circus Clown's hair in black makes a funky disco hairdo.

Smooth Moves

The Disco Dude never misses an opportunity to strut. Even when he is walking down a street, he does so to his own beat!

That sparkling smile says, "Let's boogie!"

Mini Facts

Likes: The 1970s

Dislikes: Punk rock music

See Also: Hula Dancer (S3), Flamenco Dancer (S6)

Did You Know?

The Disco Dude's memorable outfit was inspired by many different 1970s disco references.

Wide lapels, polyester suits, and big gold medallions are what the 1970s were all about

Pop Star

A singing sensation at the top of the charts

A RUN OF BIG HIT songs has made the Pop Star one of the biggest musical celebrities in the world. She may travel by limo and private jet, and have her own fan club, but deep down she is just a regular Minifigure. What she loves most is the music. She still hangs out with her old friends, and loves to sing in front of the mirror.

Microphone's top is textured just like the real thing

A Hit Hairstyle

The Pop Star isn't just here to debut her latest single; she also premieres a brand-new hair piece and microphone accessory.

Pink and silver are the Pop Star's favorite colors

Mini Facts

Likes: Singing her heart out

Dislikes: Losing her voice

See Also: Rapper (S3), Rocker Girl (S7)

Did You Know?

The Pop Star was created in honor of then-Creative Director Matthew Ashton's love of pop music.

YOU GO, GIRL!

Series 3

5+
8803
LEGO minifigures

JANUARY 2011 The third series of Minifigures introduced a grass skirt, baseball gear, and a long-awaited Elf to the ever-expanding lineup. It also included the first in a bizarre and beloved set of characters dressed in animal costumes.

Pilot

Tribal Chief

I FEEL A LITTLE UNDERDRESSED....

Sumo Wrestler

Hula Dancer

Fisherman

Samurai Warrior

Space Alien

Rapper

Samurai Warrior

A seriously skilled swordsman

THE SAMURAI WARRIOR is famous for his skill with the sword and his sense of responsibility. He never breaks a promise or refuses to help someone in need, and he will accept no greater reward than a cup of hot tea. His only flaw is that he has absolutely no sense of humor.

Sword is the same as the Ninja's, but in a different color

Did You Know?

Armor-covered minifigure torsos are often left blank, but this time the LEGO® designers decided to go all-out with printed decoration.

Mini Facts

Likes: Being responsible

Dislikes: Knock-knock jokes

See Also: Ninja (S1), Kimono Girl (S4), Heroic Knight (S9)

Armor and samurai helmet originally come from classic LEGO® Ninjago sets

Plated skirt protects upper legs

Guardian's Garb

Beneath his armor, the Samurai Warrior wears a traditional "obi" (sash) and a patterned cotton suit called a "yoroi hitatare".

46

IT'S ALWAYS GOOD TO MEET ANOTHER NOBLE WARRIOR!

Sumo Wrestler

A health-conscious heavyweight

THE SUMO WRESTLER has been nicknamed "The Immovable Object" for his ability to stand still while his opponent tries to push him out of the ring. Although his career depends on maintaining a certain body size, he always eats a proper diet, finishes his vegetables, and says, "Thank you", when he is done.

New hair piece with topknot

Did You Know?

The Sumo Wrestler is definitely the LEGO Minifigures character with the least amount of clothes (not counting robots).

Title Bout

The Sumo Wrestler and the Super Wrestler had a match once, but it ended in a tie. The Sumo Wrestler could not beat the Super Wrestler's moves, but the Super Wrestler could not make the Sumo Wrestler budge!

Printed details add extra girth

Mawashi wrestling belt

Mini Facts

Likes: Broccoli

Dislikes: Sore losers

See Also: Super Wrestler (S1), Lawn Gnome (S4)

Space Alien

A would-be world conqueror and reluctant tourist

THE SPACE ALIEN arrived to take over the planet with a map of Earth and an Alien-to-Human dictionary, but neither one works very well. It is hard to take over the world when no one understands what you say and you can't find any important locations, so the out-of-sorts extraterrestrial has started touring roadside attractions instead.

First character in the LEGO Minifigures series to have a non-standard head shape

Complex breathing system for surviving in Earth's atmosphere

???

Translation Error

The Space Alien does not understand the Minifigures it meets on Earth, but it thinks the planet is pretty awesome anyway!

Mini Facts

Likes: Giant cement squirrels

Dislikes: Language barriers

See Also: Classic Alien (S6)

Exclusive gold sci-fi blaster and purple laser beam

Space Villain

A battle-scarred veteran of villainy

THE SPACE VILLAIN has seen a lot of action in his career as a cosmic criminal. He lost an eye over Spyrius IV, misplaced a leg in the Insectoid hivefleet's meteor mines, and his right arm is somewhere at the end of a black hole. Still, he wouldn't trade his job for all the quasar rubies in the M-Tron Nebula.

Transparent yellow visor blocks solar radiation

Crooked Cyborg

The Space Villain has had many of his body parts replaced with cybernetic enhancements. Even his teeth are made of metal now.

Mini Facts

Likes: Space piracy

Dislikes: FuturonCorp security-bots

See Also: Spaceman (S1), Alien Villainess (S8)

Pressurized space suit

Peg leg from 1989 LEGO® Pirates theme

Did You Know?

The Space Villain has many references to classic LEGO® Space themes. The green "B" on his chest is the 1991 logo of the villainous Blacktron armada (which originally premiered in 1987).

Fisherman

A storyteller whose tall tales are all true

THE FISHERMAN is full of stories of the sea, like the time he caught a school of flying fish with a butterfly net, or when he hooked a giant squid but had to throw it back because it wasn't giant squid season. No one believes his unlikely tales, which is too bad, because every one of them really happened.

Fish attaches to end of line—no hook required

New short beard element

New fishing rod with removable reel and string

Waterproof fishing waders

Mini Facts

Likes: Telling stories

Dislikes: Not being believed

See Also: Lawn Gnome (S4), Ice Fisherman (S5)

And Under The Beard...

If you happen to lose the Fisherman's beard, don't worry—he's got another one underneath! Maybe this is what he looked like when he was a little younger.

Did You Know?

Although a LEGO fishing pole already existed, the Fisherman's rod was redesigned to fit into a LEGO Minifigures series bag.

50

Snowboarder

A confident athlete who loves the cold

THE SNOWBOARDER is happiest when the wind blows and the temperature drops. She travels to the coldest places in the world, and moves on as soon as the weather starts to warm up. As long as there is snow on the ground, she and her board can do just about anything.

Helmet with flip-up goggles

New snowboard can be held by a minifigure hand

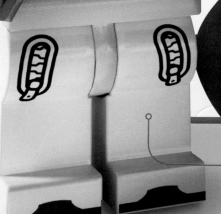

Outfit keeps the Snowboarder cozy in the coldest climates

Boards For All Seasons

Skateboards, surfboards, and snowboards...the LEGO Minifigures line has something for every kind of boarder!

Did You Know?

The Snowboarder was originally planned as a male minifigure, but extreme sports seemed like the perfect fit for a lady with attitude. A male version would follow in Series 5.

Mini Facts

Likes: Cold temperatures

Dislikes: Summer heat

See Also: Skier (S2), Snowboarder Guy (S5), Downhill Skier (S8)

Tennis Player

A fierce competitor who plays to win

THE TENNIS PLAYER streaks across the tennis court, dashing to and fro to strike the ball with absolute precision and perfect aim at every swing. With her one-of-a-kind lucky racket that was forged from meteorite alloy on a mountain top by a master racket-smith, she is convinced that she'll never lose a match!

New tennis racket accessory

Ponytail keeps hair out of face during matches

Mini Facts

Likes: Winning

Dislikes: Tying

See Also: Tennis Ace (S7)

Pleated skirt for maximum mobility

Did You Know?

This was the first tennis racket and tennis player to be produced by the LEGO Group.

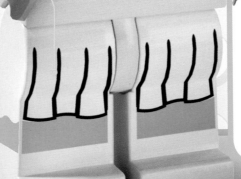

World Of Sports

From hockey players to tennis aces, the world of LEGO Minifigures is filled with sport-loving athletes. Whether they are team players or solo acts, these miniature champions always keep in shape and play their best!

Baseball Player

A team player who loves the game

THE BASEBALL PLAYER really loves to play the sport well. He does his best to help his team by learning strategies and paying attention to his coach's signals, and he always tries to give the fans in the stands a game to remember. He also collects vintage baseball-stadium hot dogs!

Baseball bat is made of white plastic, but the end is painted brown, so the color won't rub off the handle

New cap element with curved brim

Mini Memorabilia

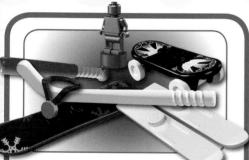

Past LEGO® Sports themes include Soccer, Basketball and Hockey. When new sports were introduced into the LEGO Minifigures line, new accessories had to be designed to go with them!

Classic pinstriped baseball uniform

Did You Know?

The Baseball Player's team is called the Clutchers, named for the clutch mechanism that allows LEGO bricks to hold together.

Mini Facts

Likes: Good teamwork

Dislikes: Striking out

See Also:
Baseball Fielder (S10)

In The Caves

YOU NEVER KNOW what you will find when you go exploring in the LEGO® world. A deep, dark cavern might be home to cave people from the prehistoric past, or it could be a meeting place for lots of spooky monsters!

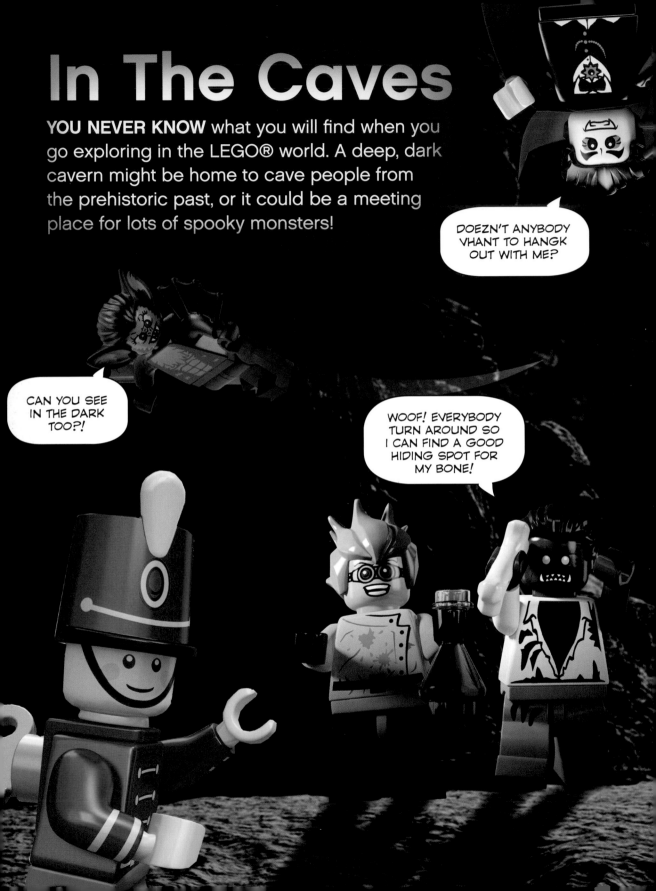

Rapper

A gold-plated genius of the well-timed rhyme

THE RAPPER has become very skilled at coming up with clever rhymes for his rap songs. He has found fame through his abilty to come up with words that sound alike, even ones that everyone else says are impossible. He once won a prize for finding a rhyme for "orange!"

Gold cap

Golden Ambition

The Rapper's rhymes have made him so rich that he has had most of his belongings plated with gold—even his teeth! Don't tell the Conquistador.

Did You Know?

Thanks to his low-slung jeans, the Rapper has the honor of being the first LEGO minifigure with his underwear showing.

Gold teeth

Gold medallion

Gold-trimmed boombox

Gold microphone

Mini Facts

Likes: Complicated rhymes

Dislikes: Forgetting the words

See Also: Pop Star (S2)

> ARE YOU GUYS HEADING TO THE PARTY?

Hula Dancer

A musical Minifigure who dances all day long

THERE'S JUST something about being out in the tropical sun that makes the Hula Dancer want to move to a beat. She knows all of the ancient and modern hula dances and is happy to teach them to anybody who wants to learn. If you hear music on a bright sunny day, you can bet that she is right there dancing.

Did You Know?

Although the Hula Dancer's hair piece isn't new, this is the first time it has a printed decoration.

Tropical flower in hair

A Special Skirt

Made of a material similar to the minifigure cape, the Hula Dancer's grass skirt is folded into shape and held by the pegs that attach her legs to her torso.

Coconut maracas

Hawaiian flower garland

Mini Facts

Likes: Music, dancing

Dislikes: Cloudy days

See Also: Flamenco Dancer (S6)

Tribal Chief

A great seeker of adventure

THE TRIBAL CHIEF lives for adventure. If there is a mountain, he will climb it. If there is a river, he will swim it. If there is a desert, he will hike across it—just to prove to himself that he can. He loves the great outdoors, especially when he can bring his friends along on the adventure too!

Each feather was earned by an act of bravery or a good deed

A broad smile to show his bold and adventurous spirit

A Frozen Journey

The Tribal Chief once decided to walk all the way to the South Pole. He just wanted to see if he could do it!

Beaded chest piece is both armor and ornamentation

Did You Know?

The Tribal Chief's headdress is highly decorated, down to the tips of the eagle feathers and his painted hair in the back.

Mini Facts

Likes: Wilderness challenges

Dislikes: Sudden hailstorms

See Also: Explorer (S2)

Race Car Driver

A wild racer with a need for speed

YEARS AGO, the Race Car Driver met a man with a robot monkey who told him that he would be compelled to seek out great speeds all of his life. The prediction came true, and now that he is a professional racing driver, he can tour the world's racetracks in the fastest four-wheeled vehicles ever built.

No Helmet-Hair

Like the Magician, the Race Car Driver comes with an alternate hair piece for when he is not wearing his helmet.

Racing helmet with flip-up visor and classic LEGO Octan gasoline logo

Flying wrench logo on jacket

"Stafford Engines" sponsor is named after designer Mark Stafford

THE RACE TRACK IS ONE THING, BUT WATCH YOUR SPEED ON MY STREETS, PAL!

Did You Know?

The Race Car Driver's jacket is loaded with references, including the name of designer Nik Groves, who hadn't yet obtained his driver's license.

Mini Facts

Likes: No speed limits

Dislikes: Running out of gas

See Also: Skater (S1), Roller Derby Girl (S9)

Pilot

An old-time airman who's flown it all

THE PILOT has been flying for longer than anybody else can remember. Biplanes, triplanes, sea planes, and jet planes—if it has wings, then he has steered it through the skies in his time. On his historic travels, he has discovered lost mountaintop civilizations, faced sabotaging gremlins, and even battled against invading Moon Men!

Old-fashioned aviator's cap with movable goggles

Mini Facts

Likes: Strong tailwinds

Dislikes: Retirement

See Also: Skydiver (S10), Sea Captain (S10), Grandpa (S10)

Of all his missions, the Pilot's proudest achievement is growing his fine mustache

Warm collar for icy high altitudes

Pilot's Pack

A traveling knapsack doubles as a parachute pack for the Pilot! It comes in handy when he needs to make a daring excape.

Did You Know?
The Pilot is a homage to classic pilots and adventurers featured in British fiction.

Mummy

A monster who knows 1,000 curses

WATCH OUT, or the Mummy might put an ancient curse on you. He loves to make people wake up with their beds full of slimy frogs, or find their shoelaces tied together, or always have their toast land butter-side-down. He doesn't do it to be mean—he just thinks that is what mummies are supposed to do.

Creepy glowing eyes

Wrinkly mummy skin peeking through wrappings

Creepy Cousins

The Zombie and the Mummy get along well...In a way, isn't a Mummy just a really old and well-preserved Zombie?

Did You Know?

The Mummy has more painted decoration than most of the Minifigures. His bandages appear on his front, the sides of his arms and legs, and even his back.

Mini Facts

Likes:
An air-conditioned coffin

Dislikes: Sand in his bandages

See Also: Pharaoh (S2), Egyptian Queen (S5)

Stinging scorpion pal

WITH ALL OF THOSE BANDAGES, I THOUGHT YOU WERE ONE OF MY PATIENTS!

Elf

A legendary warrior of the mystic woodlands

THE ELF'S skill with the longbow and his ability to scout in the wilderness can not be equaled. Dwelling in the remote and forbidden Elflands, north of the Western Kingdom, he can walk across dry leaves without a rustle and leap through the treetops with astounding agility. He is also pretty good at writing epic poetry!

The Ears Have It

The Elf has a number of new parts and accessories, but the most exciting for collectors was his hair piece, complete with painted, pointy elf ears—a minifigure debut!

Mini Facts

Likes: Playing the panpipes

Dislikes: Evil wizards

See Also: Evil Dwarf (S5), Heroic Knight (S9)

Did You Know? A 2008 issue of the official LEGO® Club magazine included a reference to elves on an illustrated LEGO Castle map, but it wasn't until 2011 that the first Elf minifigure finally arrived.

New longbow weapon is larger and more elegantly curved than the standard LEGO bow

Elvish cloak is enchanted against rain, cold, and dragon's breath

New shield decorated with a stag symbol

Gorilla Suit Guy

A peculiar person who has gone totally ape

THE GORILLA SUIT GUY is baffling. Who is he? Why is he wearing that costume? Does he think he is an actual gorilla? He certainly acts like one whenever he is spotted at the park or zoo. And while it is quite obvious that he is not a real gorilla, somehow no one wants to be the one to tell him that!

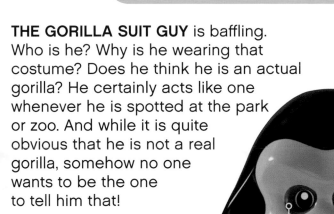

Holes match up with minifigure eyes underneath

With his mask on, the only giveaway that this is a costume is the zipper printed on his back

Hot Jungle

Take off the Gorilla Suit Guy's mask and you are in for a surprise. It looks like it's very hot inside that suit!

Bananas are Gorilla Suit Guy's favorite snack

Mini Facts

Likes: Bananas, hooting, scratching

Dislikes: Being called a monkey

See Also: Lizard Man (S5), Zookeeper (S5)

Did You Know?

The Gorilla Suit Guy is the first of a number of LEGO Minifigures characters who wear animal costumes. He is also the only one so far with a mask that covers his whole face (except for the eyes).

Series 4

APRIL 2011 The fourth series was full of firsts: the first use of shorter legs on a LEGO® Minifigures character; the first-ever minifigure mohawk hairstyle, and the first appearance of revisited character types with the line's second surfer and skateboarder!

Sailor

Werewolf

Kimono Girl

Lawn Gnome

I'M GOING TO SKATE RIGHT OFF THIS PAGE!

Street Skater

Hockey Player

Hazmat Guy

Musketeer

Musketeer

A charming swordsman seeking a worthy rival

THE MUSKETEER has combed the world for anyone who can match his skill with a blade. All he wants is a good challenge, but no one has even come close to equaling his dazzling swordsmanship. Thus, after a smile, a bow, and a handshake for each defeated opponent, he sets off to seek his next duel.

The Musketeer always keeps his uniform neat and clean

New cup hilt sword was designed so it could also be used as an antenna in LEGO® models

Mini Facts

Likes: Big hats with feathers

Dislikes: Poor sportsmanship

See Also: Samurai Warrior (S3), Highland Battler (S6), Heroic Knight (S9)

French fleur-de-lis symbol

The Dashing Duelist

The Musketeer's shortest duel ever was with the clumsy Ninja. It only lasted two seconds before the Ninja tripped and dropped his sword.

Did You Know?

Although historical musketeers were named for the musket guns they used in battle, this Musketeer was inspired by fictional stories featuring sword-wielding heroes.

YARR! I CALL DIBS ON THE NEXT DUEL MATEY!

Street Skater

A daredevil on wheels from the city streets

AS FAR as the Street Skater is concerned, the city is one big skate park. His amazing stunts take him up stairs, down trees, through fountains, and across fences, his feet never touching the ground! And his skateboard leaps and spins like it has a mind of its own!

"Brick graffiti" logo on hat

Being nearsighted doesn't stop the Street Skater from doing stunts

Did You Know?

The Street Skater's T-shirt features a glimpse of Middlesbrough Transporter Bridge from designer Michael Patton's hometown in the UK. The skyline on his skateboard is design lead Tara Wike's home city of Boston, USA.

In The Hood

Like the Series 1 Skater, the Street Skater wears a hooded sweatshirt, but his version has the hood painted on the back.

Skateboard with custom city paint job

Mini Facts

Likes: Impossible stunts

Dislikes: Flocks of pigeons

See Also: Skater (S1), Skater Girl (S6)

Artist

A painter who views the whole world as his canvas

EVERYTHING THE ARTIST sees inspires him to paint. He doesn't always carry a blank canvas with him though. He often has to make do with whatever flat surfaces are handy, such as rocks, bridges, and buildings. You'd think it might get him into trouble, but his works are so spectacular that nobody minds!

Painting great artwork requires concentration

Still Life

The Kimono Girl is one of the painter's favorite subjects. She can hold the same pose for days!

Mini Facts

Likes: Things that stay still

Dislikes: Flapping hummingbirds

See Also: Decorator (S10), Paintball Player (S10)

New paintbrush accessory

New palette for mixing colors

Did you know?

The Artist's expression was inspired by Tara Wike's husband (and fellow LEGO designer) Jason Ralls.

Paint-spattered artist's smock and trousers

I'D BE PERFECT FOR A LIFE-SIZED PORTRAIT!

Kimono Girl

A modern girl with a classic look

THE KIMONO GIRL has a deep respect for tradition. She carefully studies exactly how to wear her traditional kimono robe, how to apply her traditional white makeup, and even the proper way to hold her traditional folding fan. The only thing she loves more than traditional dress is composing haiku poetry.

"Kanzashi" hair ornament

Fan for dancing

Did You Know?

The Kimono Girl uses the Sumo Wrestler's hair with a new printed decoration, making it the only hair piece to be shared by both a male and a female character in the LEGO Minifigures line.

Pale rice powder makeup

Traditional flower pattern on kimono

Beautiful Bow

The Kimono Girl's back is printed with the elaborately folded bow which is used to tie her robe's sash, or "obi".

Mini Facts

Likes: Watching cherry blossoms fall

Dislikes: Sweeping them up afterwards

See Also: Samurai Warrior (S3), Hula Dancer (S3)

Sailor

A skilled seafarer who knows the ocean

THE SAILOR has spent his whole life at sea, so he knows every tide like the back of his hand. He can always be counted on to stay calm and steady in a nautical crisis, just like he always counts on the sea to carry him safely home at the end of each voyage.

Cap worn at a jaunty angle

Some consider it lucky to touch a sailor's striped collar

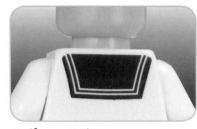

Sailor Suit

The Sailor's smartly pressed naval uniform is complete down to the oversized collar on the back.

The Sailor has a permanently squinting eye after years of peering through his telescope

Mini Facts

Likes: A well-run ship

Dislikes: Tinned sardines

See Also: Mermaid (S9), Sea Captain (S10)

Did You Know?

The Sailor is currently the only minifigure with a winking expression in the LEGO Minifigures line!

Surfer Girl

A high-spirited lover of big waves

THE SURFER GIRL likes everything about the water, from the biggest sandy beach to the tiniest tropical fish. She enjoys just dipping her toes in the surf, but she adores being up on her board riding the highest waves she can find, whooping at the top of her lungs to tell the whole ocean how much fun she is having.

Wave symbol is similar to Deep Sea Diver's

Two Of A Kind

Just like human beings, some LEGO Minifigures share the same job or hobby. Each one usually has a different take on the subject—just compare the Surfer's easy-going beachwear with the Surfer Girl's professional wetsuit!

Sleeveless wetsuit keeps arms free for balancing

Did You Know?

The Surfer Girl's surfboard (like the Surfer's) can be held by its edge in a minifigure hand.

Mini Facts

Likes: Aquariums

Dislikes: Deserts

See Also: Deep Sea Diver (S1), Surfer (S2)

Pink flames on surfboard for extra surfing speed

Punk Rocker

A riotous rebel who keeps things LOUD

IF THE PUNK ROCKER'S electric guitar is in his hands, then you can be sure that he is playing it at the highest possible volume. Some say that he was once shy and quiet until he was struck by a bolt of lightning. Others claim that he thinks his music will create world peace, just as long as it is loud enough for everyone to hear.

New electric guitar accessory

Tattered shirt collar

The Hair Up There

The Punk Rocker comes with the first-ever LEGO mohawk hair piece, produced in a softer plastic than most minifigure hair to make it flexible.

Blue jeans held together with safety pins

Mini Facts

Likes: Car alarms, explosions

Dislikes: Telephone on-hold music

See Also: Rocker Girl (S7), Bagpiper (S7)

KIDS THESE DAYS DON'T KNOW ABOUT REAL MUSIC... LIKE DISCO!

Did You Know?

The design on the Punk Rocker's T-shirt is based on a tattoo sported by designer Michael Patton.

Viking

A bold warrior on a quest to battle monsters

THE VIKING was raised on heroic ballads about his ancestors, who defended their villages from sea serpents, dragons, and fierce forest trolls. He'd love a song to be written about his own courageous battles, but no matter how hard he looks, he just can't find any monsters to fight.

Chainmail armor under sheepskin vest

Mini Facts

Likes: Listening to stories

Dislikes: Hard-to-find monsters

See Also: The Monster (S4), Viking Woman (S7)

Vikings Return

Previously seen in the 2005 LEGO Vikings theme, Viking characters have since featured in two LEGO® Minifigures series so far, including the first female member of the clan in Series 7.

Did You Know?

There's actually no evidence that Viking warriors ever wore horned helmets, but they are such well-known accessories that the LEGO designers included them.

Decorated shield provides protection against a troll's club

Short-handled battle-ax

At The Circus

EVERY MINIFIGURE has a special talent and where better to show it off than under a colorful Minifigure tent? The circus isn't just for clowning around—everybody gets a turn at putting on an amazing show!

AIN'T NOBODY CAN TWIRL A LASSO LONGER'N ME.

OOPS. ERM... LOOKS LIKE I'M GOING TO NEED ANOTHER VOLUNTEER!

DID SOMEBODY SAY THEY WANTED PIE?

Ice Skater

A graceful skater and imaginative sculptress

THE ELEGANT ICE SKATER can create a figure-skating routine for any type of music, but it is another talent that has catapulted her to stardom. At the end of her performance, she rises onto a giant block of ice and, in a dazzling display of leaps and pirouettes, uses her skates to carve it into a magnificent ice sculpture!

New upswept hair piece

Mini Facts

Likes: Fancy hairstyles

Dislikes: Running out of hairspray

See Also: Hockey Player (S4), Ice Fisherman (S5)

Different arm colors for an asymmetric, single sleeved dress

Did You Know?

The Ice Skater's silver skates are one of the smallest pieces created for the LEGO Minifigures line.

Bottom half of her gown is made of fabric to allow figure skating poses

Sparkling On The Ice

The Ice Skater is covered with silver sparkles on both sides of her skating costume and even on her face. Look closely and you'll see that some are dots and others are stars.

New ice skates attached to feet

Soccer Player

A good sportsman with a head for goals

THE SOCCER PLAYER may not win every game he plays, but he leads his team with sportsmanship, skill, and a smile. This sports star is a fast runner, a precise goal scorer, and he has knocked so many balls into the goal with his head, he has lost count of how many times he has scored.

Same brick logo as the Weightlifter

Base of trophy is made from a LEGO fez hat piece

Mini Facts

Likes: A great match

Dislikes: Rough play

See Also: Baseball Player (S3), Football Player (S8)

Shield with team symbol

Octan sponsorship logo

Did You Know?

The fictional brand Octan is the official gasoline for LEGO autos everywhere, and the sponsor of the Soccer Player's team, the Brick Kickers.

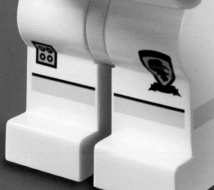

Gold, Silver And Bronze

Collect the Karate Master, Soccer Player, and Sumo Wrestler, and you will have trophies for first, second, and third place.

Crazy Scientist

A creator whose inventions are never quite evil enough

THE CRAZY SCIENTIST has been trying for years to create the perfect wacky science project. He has got everything he needs—a creepy old laboratory, lots of bubbling beakers and machinery, and even a lightning rod—but somehow his evil inventions always turn out nice. He can't figure out why, and it is driving him crazy!

Hair stands on end from one too many electric jolts

An Experiment Gone Wrong

The Crazy Scientist designed The Monster to wreak havoc and terrify the citizens. How was he supposed to know his evil creation would be friendly and helpful instead?

Chemical-stained lab coat

Night-vision lab goggles in case of power failure

Did You Know?

The Crazy Scientist's new laboratory flask accessory is made of clear and transparent green plastic molded together.

Mini Facts

Likes: Building the perfect monster

Dislikes: Failure

See Also: The Monster (S4), Mr. Good and Evil (S9)

DID SOMEBODY INVENT ME? I WONDER WHAT I WAS BUILT TO DO?

The Monster

A creature with a scary face and a heart of gold

DON'T JUDGE THE MONSTER by his appearance. He is actually one of the nicest LEGO Minifigures around. Whenever he sees somebody having trouble moving a heavy object, he runs right over to help. And if his colossal strength means that he accidentally smashes it or throws it into orbit... everybody knows he meant well.

Clothes often torn during feats of strength

The Band-Aids on The Monster's forehead are designed to make him look more silly than frightening!

Head For A Hat

The Monster's high-up cranium was created by making a new hat-like piece that could fit over the top of a normal minifigure head.

Mini Facts

Likes: Helping people

Dislikes: Torches and pitchforks

See Also: Mummy (S3), Clockwork Robot (S6)

The Crazy Scientist is not known for his neat needlework

Hockey Player

A real animal on the ice

RAISED BY a pack of wolves out on the frozen tundra, the Hockey Player was discovered by a traveling sports agent and recruited into the even wilder world of professional ice hockey. Whether he is chasing the puck or fiercely guarding his home goal, no player is more loyal to his team.

New face guard snaps onto classic helmet piece

Mini Facts

Likes: Raw meat

Dislikes: Taking a bath

See Also:
Werewolf (S4),
Football
Player (S8)

Padded armor for tough impacts on ice

First ever hockey stick element (the LEGO Hockey minifigures held bars instead)

A Ferocious Figure

Whatever you do, don't take the Hockey Player's steak away before he's done with it. That guard on his helmet isn't just for his own protection!

1x1 LEGO roundplate used for a puck

80

Werewolf

A furry beast who's more tame than terrifying

THE LIGHT of the full moon unleashes a startling transformation, changing an ordinary LEGO Minifigure into a wolf-like beast. But instead of rampaging through the countryside, the Werewolf prefers to romp in the park, fetch sticks, and dig holes in yards. He isn't very frightening, but he'd appreciate it if you would act scared anyway.

Moonlight Mishap

The Werewolf loves to bury his chew-bone, but he always forgets where he hid it.

Clothes shredded during transformation

This bone is the Werewolf's favorite object in the entire world

Extremely sensitive sense of smell

Did You Know?

The LEGO designers love to create pieces that have multiple uses. A single new hair piece provides two very different looks for the Series 3 Elf and the Werewolf.

Mini Facts

Likes: Howling, playing catch

Dislikes: Fleas

See Also: Minotaur (S6), Vampire Bat (S8)

Lawn Gnome

A little minifigure with a lot of patience

AS LONG as the Lawn Gnome has something nice to look at, he can stay in the same position for years and years. Just don't mistake him for a statue and move him to a less interesting spot, because if he doesn't like the view, he'll pack up his fishing pole and be on his way.

First appearance of fishing pole in brown

Fables And Folklore

Several LEGO Minifigures have their roots in mythology and fairy tales. The Lawn Gnome serves both as a fantasy creature and a garden decoration!

Mini Facts

Likes: People watching

Dislikes: Moss

See Also: Fisherman (S3), Leprechaun (S6)

The Lawn Gnome shares his bushy beard and fondness for fishing with the series 3 Fisherman

New pointed green hat element

Did You Know?

The Lawn Gnome was the first character in the LEGO Minifigures line to have shorter minifigure legs. Just don't be cheeky and mention it to him!

Hazmat Guy

A clean-up expert whose job makes him a little nervous

THE HAZMAT Guy is who you call after an alien invasion or a giant mutant attack. He has dealt with every kind of glowing goo imaginable, and with the help of his protective suit and gear, he gets everything cleaned up like new. Dealing with so many weird emergencies has made him pretty jittery, though.

Suit features rarely used flame-orange color

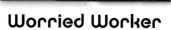

Worried Worker

In a world of crazy scientists, lizard men, aliens, and evil robots, the Hazmat Guy really has his work cut out for him!

Airtight suit protects against hazardous materials

International radiation warning symbol

Did You Know?

The Hazmat Guy was originally planned to feature in an earlier series, but his helmet was so complex to mold and assemble that he had to be delayed!

Suction and dispersal gear plugs into the back of his suit

Mini Facts

Likes: Peace and quiet

Dislikes: Weird smells

See Also: Crazy Scientist (S4), Lizard Man (S5)

Series 5

AUGUST 2011 Series 5 took a tour around the world with characters from locations including Great Britain, the Arctic, ancient Egypt, and the gladiatorial pits of Rome. New accessories included ten new pieces of hair and headgear alone!

Graduate

Egyptian Queen

SOMETHING'S DEFINITELY FISHY OVER HERE...

Detective

Royal Guard

I'VE CAUGHT A BIG ONE!

WOULD YOU LIKE TO TAKE A CLOSER LOOK AT MY PIE...

Fitness Instructor

Ice Fisherman

Small Clown

Boxer

Gangster

A villain with a little police problem

THE GANGSTER has a problem. All he wants is to sneak around the city robbing banks and setting up money-making scams, but the LEGO® world is filled with police officers and other do-gooders. Whenever he manages to start up a profitable crime, a hero always shows up to save the day and he has to run away again.

Did You Know?

The Gangster's violin case is designed to open up so he can conceal his pistol inside. What a crook!

Evil hat

Evil pencil-thin mustache

Evil expensive suit

Mini Facts

Likes: Stealing money

Dislikes: Getting caught

See Also: Space Villain (S3), Bandit (S6)

Evil trick violin case

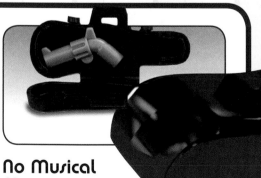

No Musical Maestro

Will there ever be a LEGO violin to go in this case? Only time will tell...and the Gangster isn't saying!

Detective

A sleuth whose solutions take more than sheer luck

THE CLEVER DETECTIVE
has never met a mystery that he couldn't solve. No matter how impossible the case may appear, he just whips out his magnifying glass and follows the clues until he discovers the correct answer. Ask him how he does it and he will tell you that it is all "elementary".

New deerstalker cap with decorated earflaps on the sides

Weatherproof topcoat

Gray magnifying glass frame and handle

HEH HEH HEH!

Classic Cases
The Detective successfully solved cases include the Brickster's Baffling Brick Napping, the Sam Sinister Switcheroo, and the Mystery of Timmy's Nose—all references to earlier LEGO themes.

Mini Facts

Likes: Mystery novels

Dislikes: Math problems

See Also: Policeman (S9) Mr. Good and Evil (S9)

Did You Know?
With his deerstalker hat and magnifying glass, it's no surprise to learn that the Detective was inspired by another famous fictional mystery-solver.

CAN YOU DETECT WHERE THE PARTY IS?

Lizard Man

A minifigure with an appetite for imaginary destruction

WHEN YOU DREAM of being a giant monster, what do you do? The Lizard Man decided to make himself a lizard costume and build a bunch of tiny cars and buildings out of his bricks. Now he can smash his way through the city streets as much as he wants.

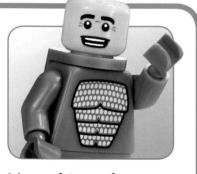

Lizard Laughs

He may not be crushing real cities, but beneath his removable monster mask, the Lizard Man is clearly having a great time.

Pointy spikes

Mini Facts

Likes: Roaring and stomping

Dislikes: Bricks between his toes

See Also: Gorilla Suit Guy (S3), Bunny Suit Guy (S7), Chicken Suit Guy (S9)

Tail running along his back is attached at the neck

Indestructable stomach scales

Did You Know?

The Lizard Man is the first minifigure to have a molded tail.

Zookeeper

An animal lover in a world of very strange beasts

THE ZOOKEEPER has loved animals ever since the first time she visited the monkey enclosure at the zoo. She knows how to feed and take proper care of every species. Luckily for her, the LEGO world includes everything from camels and frogs to dinosaurs, dragons, and rock monsters.

OOH OOH!

Odd Ape

The Zookeeper once met the Gorilla Suit Guy, but she wasn't quite sure what to do with him!

Did You Know?

The Zookeeper's chimpanzee can be attached to a brick stud, or its arm can be held by a clip or minifigure hand. Bar-shaped pieces (like the stem of a banana) can also fit between its open hand and the top of its head.

Mini Facts

Likes: Taking care of animals

Dislikes: Watching hippos eat

See Also: Explorer (S2) Jungle Boy (S7)

A tasty banana treat is a great way to get a chimp to behave

New baby chimpanzee element with painted face and ears

Lumberjack

A rugged man of the rugged woods

A TRUE MINIFIGURE of the outdoors, the Lumberjack builds his own log cabins, cooks his own stews, brews his own maple syrup, and avoids the big city as much as possible. He is pretty hard-headed, which comes in handy when the trees he chops down with his ax fall in the wrong direction!

New ax element with painted head

Cap with a beaver logo

Clad In Plaid

The Lumberjack's intricate plaid shirt patterning is printed on his arms, and the front and back of his torso.

Mini Facts

Likes: Being tough and self-reliant

Dislikes: Splinters

See Also: Forest Maiden (S9), Tomahawk Warrior (S10)

Rough beard stubble like sandpaper

Warm flannel shirt

Did You Know?

The "Kel" on the Lumberjack's shirt is for Kel Henson, a Canadian LEGO fan whose favorite animal is the beaver.

NICE AX. BUT MINE'S BETTER!

Evil Dwarf

A wicked warrior who is sensitive about his whiskers

THE EVIL DWARF'S bristly black beard has been his pride and joy ever since he was a lad living in the Dwarven Kingdom. Now that he has grown up, he has turned into a mean-tempered bully. Make fun of his beard and you had better run away as fast as you can.

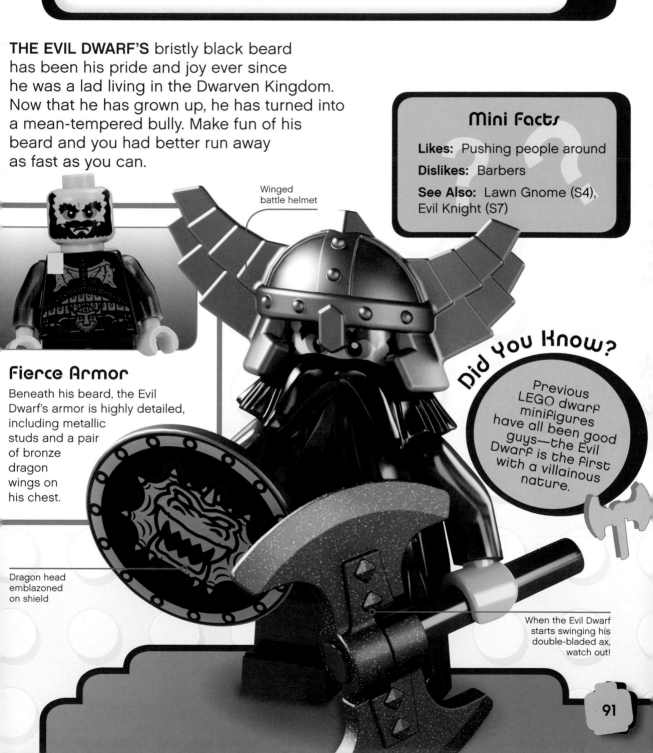

Winged battle helmet

Mini Facts

Likes: Pushing people around

Dislikes: Barbers

See Also: Lawn Gnome (S4), Evil Knight (S7)

Fierce Armor

Beneath his beard, the Evil Dwarf's armor is highly detailed, including metallic studs and a pair of bronze dragon wings on his chest.

Dragon head emblazoned on shield

Did You Know?

Previous LEGO dwarf minifigures have all been good guys—the Evil Dwarf is the first with a villainous nature.

When the Evil Dwarf starts swinging his double-bladed ax, watch out!

91

Gladiator

A champion who wants to give peace a chance

THERE ARE FEW more skilled than the mighty Gladiator at battling warriors and wild beasts. He has proven himself a champion of the arena several times, but secretly, he wishes that he could find another way to entertain an audience. Maybe he could do something that does not involve getting poked with so many pointy objects.

Murmillo fish-like gladiator helmet

Roman gladius sword

Perfect Vision

Care was taken when designing the Gladiator to make sure that his printed eyes lined up exactly with two of the small round holes in his helmet's faceplate.

Lightweight leather and bronze armor for agility

Mini Facts

Likes: Not having to fight

Dislikes: Swords, spears, clubs, tridents

See Also: Spartan Warrior (S2), Roman Soldier (S6)

Did You Know?

The Gladiator's new sword and helmet are based on equipment used by real historical gladiators.

Boxer

A prizefighter who is his own biggest fan

THE BOXER has amazed fans everywhere with his smooth moves, swift uppercuts, and punchy attitude—but his greatest fan by far is himself. No one has been able to defeat him yet, despite his endless quest for a worthy opponent. What he really wants is a cloning machine so he can box against himself.

Padded helmet and printed yellow mouth guard protect against powerful blows

Can't Win 'Em All

The Boxer was the very first character in the LEGO Minifigures line to have an alternate expression printed on the opposite side of his head.

Mini Facts

Likes: A flawless victory

Dislikes: Picking things up

See Also: Super Wrestler (S1), Karate Master (S2)

Did You Know?

The Boxer is the first minifigure to have both of his hands replaced with accessories. He is also the first to wear boxing gloves.

Gold and black championship belt

Boxing gloves rotate and pose just like minifigure hands

Most Wanted

MOST MINIFIGURES ARE FRIENDLY, but there are a few rotten eggs out to spoil everybody else's fun. Fortunately, these bad guys just aren't very good at being bad and their villainous misdeeds usually backfire with hilarious results.

HEY, YOU— READING THIS BOOK. STICK 'EM UP!

I MAY BE THREE AND A HALF CENTIMETERS TALL, BUT I'M SIX CENTIMETERS WORTH OF BAD TEMPER.

6cm

5cm

4cm

3cm

2cm

Small Clown

An entertainer who lives for big laughs

THE SMALL CLOWN works hard after every performance to make his jokes even bigger and better. He has learned every gag book by heart, subscribed to the best clowning magazines, and holds an advanced degree in Mirth from Clown University. His philosophy is that if you are not guffawing, he is not doing his job right.

New bowler hat with painted squirting flower

Unlike the Circus Clown, the Small Clown's head is entirely white

Did You Know?

The Small Clown is the second character in Series 5 to use the small-legs piece, and the third short LEGO Minifigures character produced. His bowler hat and cream pie are both new elements.

Mini Facts

Likes: Throwing pies

Dislikes: Explaining punch lines

See Also: Circus Clown (S1), Ringmaster (S2)

Who Nose?

What do the Small Clown, the Circus Clown, and the Werewolf all have in common? They are the only three characters in the LEGO Minifigures line with that rarest of features: a printed nose!

Coconut cream pie is for throwing at people, not eating!

Fitness Instructor

A trainer who wants to get everybody in great shape

WITH HER BOOMBOX full of high-energy tunes and her determination to help everybody get fit, the Fitness Instructor makes exercise look like so much fun. No one can resist joining in her routines—just be prepared for an exhausting workout. She can keep up her routine for hours.

Did You Know?

The Fitness Instructor's lavender boombox is based on a radio owned by designer Tara Wike's childhood best friend...one that she always thought was really cool!

Look-Alikes

Sometimes the Fitness Instructor and the Pop Star like to switch places for a day, just to see if anybody notices.

Sweatband to keep sweat off her face during workouts

Leg warmers help prevent cramping and muscle injuries

Mini Facts

Likes: Burning calories

Dislikes: Stopping to rest

See Also: Weightlifter (S2), Sumo Wrestler (S3)

New color for the Rapper's boombox accessory

Cave Woman

A practical lady of the prehistoric era

WHILE THE CAVEMAN is trying to invent new things, the Cave Woman is working on practical matters like creating tools, clothing, and developing a spoken language. Despite her superior brainpower, she is very fond of her lovably primitive mate and does her best to protect him from hungry meat eaters (and his own inventions).

Bone in hair might be an ornament...or leftovers

ARGH! HELP MEEE!

LOOK, A LOVELY NEW COAT.

Stone Age Garb

Like the Caveman, the Cave Woman wears clothing made of animal skins. Unlike her partner, her outfit was created with more care and taste.

Spear-head pendant (made from molten lava) was a romantic gift from her first date with the Caveman

First appearance of the spiked stone club accessory in dark brown

Mini Facts

Likes:
The Caveman

Dislikes: Chasing saber-toothed cats

See Also:
Caveman (S1)

Did You Know?

The Cave Woman's new soft-plastic hair piece has a built-in clip for attaching bones and other accessories shaped like the LEGO bar piece.

Egyptian Queen

A smart and powerful ruler

THE EGYPTIAN QUEEN may sit on a golden throne and dine on sumptuous banquets every day, but the royal life hasn't made her soft. She knows everything there is to know about tax codes, crop rotation, and politics. Even her subjects say that for an all-powerful sovereign, she is really not so bad.

Winged scarab-shaped diadem printed on hair

Did You Know?

In ancient Egypt, women of high status often wore jeweled wigs. The Egyptian Queen's new hair piece has not appeared in any other LEGO set.

Mini Facts

Likes: Being Queen

Dislikes: Criticism

See Also: Pharaoh (S2), Roman Emperor (S9)

Elegant gold and turquoise jewelry

I BUILT IT JUST FOR YOU, SWEETHEART!

A Gift Fit For A Queen

The Pharaoh has done everything he can to impress the Egyptian Queen... and so has the Roman Emperor!

The Egyptian Queen's pet asp (actually a LEGO rattlesnake)

PYRAMIDS ARE NOTHING... I CAN GIVE YOU AN ENTIRE EMPIRE!

Ice Fisherman

A Minifigure for whom extreme patience pays off

THE ICE FISHERMAN carefully chooses the right spot to drill a hole in the ice. Then he lowers his fishing line and waits…and waits…and waits. He might wait for hours, days, or even weeks, but he always catches something eventually. And the longer it takes, the better his catch turns out to be.

Fur lining for extra warmth

Inuit-style parka keeps out the Arctic chill

Fishing Tales

They may all come with the same main accessory, but the Fisherman, Lawn Gnome, and Ice Fisherman all have very different looks, jobs, and personalities.

Did You Know?

Although a winter hood element already existed, an entirely new one was designed for the Ice Fisherman's parka. Everything but the fur around the face opening is painted.

HE ONCE REELED IN MY MAGIC LAMP AFTER THREE MONTHS OF SITTING OUT IN THE COLD. THE FIRST THING HE WISHED FOR WAS A WARMER COAT!

Snowboarder Guy

A snowboarding pro with all the latest gear

THE SNOWBOARDER GUY knows all about wind speed, slope angles, and how much wax you should use on your board to get the smoothest glide. Thanks to all of that expertise, he has become the world's foremost tester of snowboarding equipment. If you have designed a new board, he is just the guy to put it through its paces.

Did You Know?

The text "48mm" printed on his board stands for 48 millimeters—the exact length of the LEGO snowboard element!

Mini Facts

Likes: Snow beneath his board

Dislikes: Snow inside his suit

See Also: Snowboarder (S3), Skier (S2), Downhill Skier (S8)

Latest ski goggles brand

The most aerodynamic jacket available

Cold Weather Club

With two snowboarders and two skiers, the snow-capped mountains of the LEGO Minifigures world are one popular winter destination!

Royal Guard

A steadfast protector of royalty

THE ROYAL GUARD is totally committed to his duty of protecting the palace. He stands at attention all day long, staring straight ahead and never stirring from his post. He has sworn never to move, react, or even speak unless danger threatens. Just don't try to poke him—he really hates that.

Tall bearskin hat

Chin strap printed on head

Ceremonial rifle is always ready, but rarely used

Stoic Sentinel

Try to distract him all you like, but the Royal Guard won't even blink. Rumor has it that he has even learned how to sleep standing up and with his eyes wide open.

Did You Know?

Although his costume is based on the famous uniform of the British Guard, the Royal Guard's hat is actually a combination of English and Danish styles.

Mini Facts

Likes: Standing perfectly still

Dislikes: Being tickled

See Also: Egyptian Queen (S5), Ocean King (S7)

Graduate

A young Minifigure with the rest of his life ahead of him

THE GRADUATE loved everything about college—his classes, his friends, his teachers, and even the long, late nights of homework and studying. He is very proud of his smart graduation gown and cap, and especially his hard-earned diploma. But he has only just realized something… now he has to get a job.

New mortarboard cap with tassel

Diploma printed on a 2x2 LEGO tile

Mini Facts

Likes: Finally graduating

Dislikes: Figuring out what to do next

See Also: Businessman (S8)

School tie and sweater worn under gown

Did You Know?

The Graduate's Certificate of Graduation is signed at the bottom by designer Martin Klotz.

Graduation Gear

The Graduate's gown is yet another new spin on a typical minifigure cape. Since it is packaged flat, it has to be folded down and creased to fit properly.

CONGRATULATIONS! HERE'S A PIE TO HELP YOU CELEBRATE!

Series 6

JANUARY 2012 Imagination and fantasy played a big role in Series 6, which introduced a wish-granting genie and his magic lamp, a mischievous leprechaun, a wind-up toy robot, and a pajama-clad sleepyhead to dream up adventures for all of them!

Lady Liberty

Bandit

Flamenco Dancer

Leprechaun

IS THIS SERIES 6, OR AM I JUST DREAMING?

Skater Girl

Sleepyhead

Intergalactic Girl

Roman Soldier

Classic Alien

An extraterrestrial who's out of the loop

HAVE YOU EVER HEARD that aliens built the pyramids, kidnapped Elvis, and invented the microwave? The Classic Alien has. He hasn't heard from his home planet since that whole Area 51 incident, so he gets all of his news from supermarket tabloids and internet blogs—and he believes everything he reads.

Large, unblinking eyes

Inhuman muscles

Mini Facts

Likes: Conspiracy theories

Dislikes: Cows

See Also: Space Alien (S3)

Space Cases

They may both come from outer space, but the Series 3 Space Alien and the Classic Alien couldn't be more different from each other. One fits the style of modern LEGO® sci-fi action themes, while the other is a bit more realistic… and a lot more creepy!

Unique white laser gun with green beam

Did You Know?

The Classic Alien was designed to resemble the aliens of U.F.O. sightings in popular culture.

Intergalactic Girl

A heroine who saves the universe twice a day

THE INTERGALACTIC GIRL'S daring space adventures are the stuff of legend. She has single-handedly saved solar systems from black holes, rescued civilizations from cosmic conquerors, and captured entire fleets of Blacktron battle cruisers. That's why her name is cheered on every planet, asteroid, and space station in the universe.

Space Adventures

The Intergalactic Girl can remove her hair and put on her helmet for expeditions into deep space.

Mini Facts

Likes: Foiling space-baddies' plans

Dislikes: Never getting a vacation

See Also: Spaceman (S1), Alien Villainess (S8)

Silver lipstick will be all the rage in the future

The first-ever pink LEGO spacesuit

Did You Know?

The Intergalactic Girl's space-suited design was inspired by the pulp science fiction of the 1970s.

WOW, INTERGALACTIC GIRL! I'M YOUR BIGGEST FAN!

Quasar zapper with blue beam

Antigravity boots

Roman Soldier

A legionary who does whatever he's told

JUST TELL the Roman Soldier what you want him to do and he'll march right off to do it without a moment's hesitation. Sometimes other Minifigures take advantage of his obedience by getting him to do their chores for them, but he doesn't mind—that's just what a Roman Soldier does.

Imperial galea (helmet) is painted metallic silver

Minifigure spear for a javelin

Troop Building

The Series 2 Spartan Warrior is not the only minifigure that collectors like to get extras of. Many fans have assembled entire legions of Roman Soldiers and other "trooper" characters.

Did You Know?

His shield and helmet are based on real Roman armor. Even the printed decorations on his shield are authentic.

Segmented plate armor made of metal strips fastened by leather

Mini Facts

Likes: Following orders

Dislikes: Deciding things on his own

See Also: Roman Emperor (S9), Roman Commander (S10)

Curved, rectangular shield

Heavy marching sandals printed on front and side of foot

Minotaur

A half-bull, half-Minifigure who's entirely lost

THE MYTHICAL MINOTAUR lurks deep within a twisting maze of tunnels known as the Labyrinth. Only the most brave or foolish heroes dare to venture inside to face his might. As for the monster himself, he'd rather be grazing on fresh grass, but he's never been able to find the way out.

Thick, shaggy hide

Looking Bullish

The Minotaur's head and chest are a single piece that attaches to a minifigure neck and fits over the top of the torso. It provides extra bulk and sculpted detail.

Did You Know?

The Minotaur's head was designed with holes to hold pre-existing LEGO cow horns that were first released in 2009.

Mini Facts

Likes: Open pastures

Dislikes: Treasure-seeking heroes

See Also: Gladiator (S5), Medusa (S10)

Hooves printed on feet

Garment of ancient Greece

Sleepyhead

A dozy fellow who just needs five more minutes

EVERY NIGHT, the Sleepyhead goes on amazing journeys through worlds of multicolored knights with lightning swords and time machines powered by historical hats. Eventually he has to rise and shine and get up out of bed…but at least he knows that more imaginative dreams will be waiting for him at bedtime!

New mussed-up hair piece

"Bed head" hair modeled after LEGO® Creator design manager Simon Kent

All Tuckered Out

With a twist of his head, you can change the Sleepyhead from yawning to sound asleep. Good night and sweet dreams!

Pajama stripes painted on the front and back of his torso, the front and sides of legs, and the sides of arms

Mini Facts

Likes: Napping, snoozing, sleeping

Dislikes: Caffeine

See Also: Santa (S8), Fairy (S8)

Did You Know?

The Sleepyhead's stuffed bear is a favorite creation of sculptor Gitte Thorsen, who designs and collects real teddy bears.

Teddy bear is his best buddy and dreamtime-adventure companion

Flamenco Dancer

A dazzling dancer who loves Spanish music

THE FLAMENCO DANCER lives for the fiery rhythm of the dance. She knows every part by heart: the singing, the guitar playing, the clapping, and most especially the dancing. Follow the music as it winds through the streets at night and you may discover her dancing there with her fan in hand.

Mini Facts

Likes: Flamenco

Dislikes: When the music ends

See Also: Maraca Man (S2), Hula Dancer (S3)

Fan movement is incorporated into dancing

Dress pattern continues on the back of torso

Frilly red flamenco dress

YO! IS THERE ROOM FOR ONE MORE IN YOUR MUSIC GROUP?

An Unlikely Quartet

Always looking for new ways to express her passion through dance, the Flamenco Dancer sometimes teams up with other musical Minifigures to combine their talents.

111

Genie

A mystical Minifigure of the enchanted lamp

RUB THE MAGIC LAMP and the Genie will pop out to grant your wish...as long as it's for LEGO bricks. He can't make you a king or find your true love, but he'll give you a great big pile of pieces to build anything you can imagine. Just don't ask him for instructions—that's another genie's department!

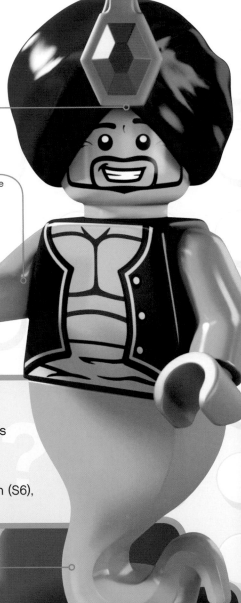

Jewel attaches to turban by a tiny peg and hole

Did You Know?

The classic LEGO turban piece was enhanced by the addition of a new jeweled ornament for the Genie.

Rare new shade of blue

The Wish Granter

The Genie's new lamp accessory is designed so that the Genie can attach on top so it looks like he's emerging from the spout.

Mini Facts

Likes: Granting wishes

Dislikes: Lack of imagination

See Also: Leprechaun (S6), Fairy (S8)

The Genie's bottom half can peg onto a LEGO brick stud

Leprechaun

An oft-pursued fable with a pot of gold

THE LEPRECHAUN is a good-humored trickster who can vanish with a wink, turn himself into an animal, or leap to the top of a tree with a single bound. His magical tricks really come in handy when people come looking for his famous pot of gold. He sometimes misplaces his treasure, but he has never lost it yet.

First decorated minifigure top hat

Three 1x1 round plates fit inside pot of gold

New pot element has bumps on its rim so that a handle can be attached

Three-leafed clover on lapel

Short Legs Club

A single piece without articulation, the short leg element was first produced in 2002 and is about three-quarters the height of standard minifigure legs.

Mini Facts

Likes: The color green

Dislikes: Rainbows (too cliché!)

See Also: Magician (S1), Lawn Gnome (S4)

Did You Know?

The Leprechaun was included in January 2012's Series 6 to make sure that he arrived in homes in time for St. Patrick's Day in March.

On Tour

GET READY for the performance of a lifetime! From rockers and rappers to pop stars and disco dancers, there are plenty of Minifigures who love to perform. Get them together and you are in for a fun-packed show.

Surgeon

A doctor who stays calm under pressure

THE SKILLFUL SURGEON keeps a level head and hand under the most extraordinary circumstances. Nothing distracts her when she's performing an important operation: not alien invasions, not giant robot attacks, and not rock monster rumblings. Of course, it's less surprising when you realize that aliens, robots, and monsters are some of her best patients.

Surgical mask keeps patients germ-free

Nerves Of Steel?
The Surgeon has to tread very carefully when treating the Football Player—he is a particularly nervous patient.

Did You Know?
The Surgeon's new scrub cap element was designed to double as a shower cap for bathing minifigures.

Surgical scrubs

Broken rib in X-ray

Blue surgical scrubs is the same rare color as the Genie

Mini Facts

Likes: Unusual patients

Dislikes: Sneezing in her mask

See Also: Nurse (S1), Skier (S2)

Mechanic

A handyman who sometimes gets carried away

NOBODY IS BETTER than the Mechanic at quick repairs, but he seldom stops there. As long as he's fixing an auto's axle, why not give it a big spoiler? And a convertible roof? And an ejector seat? And wings? By the time he's done tuning up a car, it might be a rocket ship or a submarine… or both!

New 1950s style pompadour hair piece

A Dirty Job

Unlike the spotless Surgeon, the Mechanic doesn't mind getting dirty in the course of his work.

Mini Facts

Likes: His wrench and toolbox

Dislikes: Finishing a big project

See Also: Motorcycle Mechanic (S10)

Grease stains are a badge of the job

Same flying wrench logo as the Race Car Driver

New toolbox accessory

Did You Know?

The Mechanic's "Raph" nametag is for LEGO designer Raphaël Pretesacque.

Clockwork Robot

A wind-up toy in search of his destiny

THE CLOCKWORK ROBOT started out as a simple plaything, but somewhere along the way his little ticking heart took on a life of its own. Now that he can walk and talk and think, he is trying to figure out what to do next. Maybe he'll be a cowboy...or a diver...or an astronaut.

New head element with printed eyes and mouth

TICK TOCK!

I KNOW HOW YOU FEEL!

Turn Of A Key

The Clockwork Robot's new key element attaches to a bracket piece fitted over his neck. Because it's connected by a stud, it can be turned to wind him up.

Arms built for hugging

Bright colors to resemble an old-fashioned toy

Did You Know?

The Clockwork Robot was designed to look like an old wind-up toy. His boxy new head has a stud on top for building.

Mini Facts

Likes: Hugs

Dislikes: Winding down

See Also: Robot (S1), Santa (S8)

Lady Liberty

An icon of freedom and free building

LADY LIBERTY is a symbol of creative freedom for all Minifigures. Holding her torch up high (and sometimes waving it around when she gets excited), she stands as a beacon of inspiration to all who see her, stirring the hearts of citizens everywhere to build ever greater and grander brick creations.

Did you know?

Except for her torch's flame, Lady Liberty is made entirely in one color of plastic, known as sand green.

New hair and crown element is made of soft plastic

Flame is the same piece as the Musketeer's feather

Torch is the same element as the Sailor's telescope

"JULY IV MDCCLXXVI" is printed on Lady Liberty's tablet, for July 4th, 1776—the date of the United States Declaration of Independence

Mini Facts

Likes: Imagination

Dislikes: Oppression and tyrants

See Also: Revolutionary Soldier (S10)

A Patriotic Figure

Lady Liberty is the first minifigure to be based on a real world monument: the famous Statue of Liberty in New York Harbor, USA.

NO FAIR! YOU CAN'T TURN SSSOMEONE TO SSSTONE IF THEY'RE ALREADY A SSSTATUE!

Bandit

A desperado who always cheats but never wins

THE ILL-TEMPERED, bad-mannered Bandit is a notorious outlaw of the Old West. He's an old pro at cattle-rustling, claim-jumping, and train-robbing, but his habit of taking the easy path always gets him caught by the law in the end. Whether he ends up stuck in a cactus patch or locked in jail, this cheater never prospers!

Mean eyes

The Outlaw's Grin

The Bandit usually covers his face with a bandana to conceal his identity… and keep trail dust out of his mouth.

Did You Know?

Western bad guys are often known by their black hats. The Bandit goes one better: almost his entire outfit is black, down to his uniquely colored pistols.

The Bandit may not have great aim, but he makes up for it in volume of bullets

Bandoliers are printed on back of torso, too

Mini Facts

Likes: Cheating at card games

Dislikes: Getting caught

See Also: Cowboy (S1), Cowgirl (S8)

LOOKS LIKE IT'S TIME FOR A SHOWDOWN, VARMINT!

Butcher

A friendly neighborhood purveyor of meat

THE LOCAL BUTCHER is a jolly chap, always happy to chat about the weather or pass along the latest news from town. But no matter how a conversation with him starts, it always ends up being about meat. For him, sausages, patties, and steaks aren't just an occupation—they are a way of life!

How About Some Meat?

The Minotaur and the Butcher don't really get along. Not only is the Minotaur half-cow, but he's also a vegetarian.

New T-bone steak with a convenient bone for carrying

A blue waist piece creates the effect of wrap-around apron strings

New cleaver accessory

A printed apron keeps the Butcher's clothes nice and clean

Did You Know?

The designers had some debate about the Butcher's new headwear. He almost ended up with an English trilby hat instead of a paper butcher's hat.

Mini Facts

Likes: Meat, meat products

Dislikes: Tofu

See Also: Fisherman (S3), Grandma Visitor (S7)

121

Highland Battler

A proud warrior of the Scottish Highlands

THE HIGHLAND BATTLER is proud of his fighting skills, proud of his strength, and proud of his fine plaid kilt. He believes that he is upholding the name of his clan in every challenge he faces, and he accepts nothing less than honorable victory at each one. They can take his bricks, but never his imagination!

Celtic brooch holds cloth in place

Sons Of Scotland

Although both the Highland Battler and the Bagpiper wear Scottish kilts, the Highland Battler's kilt is an older style known as a belted plaid.

An unfolded belted plaid is large enough to be used for bedding

Leather brigandine armor worn beneath kilt

Clan tartan patterning

FOR THE LAST TIME, LEPRECHAUNS ARE IRISH, NOT SCOTTISH!

Mini Facts

Likes: Winning fairly

Dislikes: Cheaters

See Also: Bagpiper (S7), Lederhosen Guy (S8)

Skater Girl

A free spirit who doesn't care what anybody thinks

SOME SKATE FOR FAME, others for thrills. But for the Skater Girl, it's all about having fun. She only cares about feeling the wind whipping through her hair and her board beneath her feet. No matter what others may think or say, she'll keep on skating—and doing everything else—her own way!

The Skater Girl is the first LEGO Minifigure with a dyed color streak in her hair

Did You Know?

The skulls on the Skater Girl's sweatshirt and skateboard are based on the head of the classic LEGO skeleton.

Third Time's The Charm

While other LEGO Minifigures sports themes have had multiple minifigures, skateboarding is the only one so far to receive three, thanks to the skaters' huge popularity among kids.

Printing on arms and back

Perky-goth fashion

Pyramid-stud belt

Mini Facts

Likes: Scary movies

Dislikes: Popularity

See Also: Skater (S1), Street Skater (S4)

123

Series 7

MAY 2012 This series matched warriors with swords, shields, spears, and blasters, with peace-loving hippies, blushing brides, a guy in a bunny suit, and a little girl with a picnic basket. It is war and peace LEGO® Minifigures style!

Bride

Daredevil

Viking Woman

Computer Programmer

CAN YOU GUYS SING BACKUP?

Rocker Girl

Aztec Warrior

Bagpiper

Galaxy Patrol

Bunny Suit Guy

A hoppy-go-lucky costumed character

NOTHING GETS the cheerful Bunny Suit Guy down. He may be unsure what a Bunny Suit Guy is or what he is supposed to do, but that doesn't stop him from hopping around town in his fuzzy costume, munching on carrots, and making people smile wherever he goes!

Did You Know!

The Bunny Suit Guy was inspired by Easter Bunny costumes. His animal outfit includes the first LEGO Minifigures mask to reveal the wearer's entire face.

New long-eared bunny hat element

The zig-zag outline around his printed tummy makes his whole costume look fuzzy

Tale Of A Tail

A round fluffy rabbit tail is printed on the back of the Bunny Suit Guy's torso.

Mini Facts

Likes: Carrot cake, carrot soup, carrot pie...

Dislikes: Angry gardeners

See Also: Gorilla Suit Guy (S3), Chicken Suit Guy (S9)

The Bunny Suit Guy's carrot is made of two separate pieces. Both the stem and the tip fit into a minifigure's hand

HELLO? CAN YOU TELL ME ABOUT THE PARTY? AW, DON'T HOP AWAY!

Rocker Girl

A glam gal who knows how much she rocks

THE ROCKER GIRL is totally confident in everything she does. She knows exactly how awesome her look and music are, and she loves showing them off in performances filled with lasers, smoke, and holograms. Whatever happens, she's always sure that her next show will be the best one yet.

New hair piece is colored for shock and styled for volume

Did You Know?

The Rocker Girl's vibrant design was inspired by the rock style of the late 1970s and early '80s. She is the first official female musician LEGO® minifigure.

Rock Duet

The Rocker Girl and the Punk Rocker may have different musical styles, but put them on stage together with their matching pink hair and guitars, and they really rock out!

Lightning-bolt makeup represents her electrifying stage presence

The Rocker Girl's favored fashions mix animal prints and solid colors

Mini Facts

Likes: Loud colors, louder music

Dislikes: Anything non-electronic

See Also: Punk Rocker (S4), DJ (S8)

Electric guitar is the same element as the Punk Rocker's, but with new color and decoration

127

Aztec Warrior

A fierce warrior of the sun

THE AZTEC WARRIOR is an elite eagle knight of the great Aztec Empire. Bearing his spear and shield, and with his eagle helmet upon his head, he battles from sunrise to sunset for the glory of his empire, defending its gold from any invaders who would dare seek to steal it away.

Ritual face paint

Bird Men

Despite how it may appear, the Aztec Warrior is not pretending to be an animal. Bird-headed helmets and feathers are a normal part of an eagle knight's uniform.

Feathered breastplate decorated with a golden mini-minifigure head

Golden battle spear

Round shield with eagle design

SAY, WOULD YOU MIND TERRIBLY IF I BORROWED SOME OF YOUR GOLD? OR ALL OF IT?

Did You Know?

To the Aztecs, the eagle was the symbol of the sun. That's why eagle knights represented the daytime, while jaguar knights represented the night.

Daredevil

A Minifigure with nerves of steel (sometimes)

THE DARING DAREDEVIL risks it all on his death-defying stunts without ever breaking a sweat. Flaming hoops and long-distance jumps over pits of snapping crocodiles are a breeze for him. It is just the everyday situations that make him nervous, like shopping for beans or buying stamps down at the post office!

Mechanic's hair piece in brown

Did You Know?

The letters "MF" on the Daredevil's belt buckle are the initials of LEGO designer Michael Fuller.

A Fearless Fellow

Thanks to his double-sided head, you can decide whether the Daredevil is triumphant... or terrified!

Stunt helmet with flip-up transparent-blue visor

Flashy red, white, and blue jumpsuit

Mini Facts

Likes: Waterskiing with sharks

Dislikes: Trying on shoes

See Also: Race Car Driver (S3), Sky Diver (S10)

Kneepads, just to be on the safe side

Galaxy Patrol

An armored defender of the galactic peace

THE GALAXY PATROL are an elite squadron of deep-space heroes sent to safeguard the most dangerous and remote sectors of the galaxy. To join, you have got to be as tough as laser nails, able to resist the mind-controlling power of a Pluuvian Brain-Beast, and capable of holding your breath in vacuum for 42 quarkoids straight!

New reinforced helmet

Mini Facts

Likes: A good laser battle

Dislikes: Dropping onto a planet from space

See Also:
Intergalactic Girl (S6), Alien Avenger (S9)

Heads-up tactical display

New heavy-duty space armor

Classic LEGO® Space logos on shoulders

Out Of Uniform

Beneath his removable chestplate, the Galaxy Patrol member wears a strength-enhancing magna-suit. His head has an orange visor print on one side and a cybernetic eye-piece on the other.

Double-barreled plasma blaster from the 2011 LEGO® Alien Conquest theme

Did You Know?

The name "LUIZ" printed on his torso is for designer Luis Castaneda.

Hippie

A flower child who makes LEGO® models, not war

THE MELLOW HIPPIE loves everything and everyone. He never stays in the same place for long, preferring to roam across the land spreading his message of peace, flower appreciation, and creativity. As a pioneer of the Free-Building movement, he believes that bricks should be assembled at random to reveal one's true inner soul as a builder.

Through The Ages

One of the best things about the LEGO Minifigures line is that its characters can come from any place...and any time!

New long hair piece with a painted headband

Tie-dyed printing on torso and arms

Flower pieces come in a set of four, leaving one extra flower in case one of them gets lost

New flower-stem piece can be held by minifigures

Did You Know?

Inspired by the peace-loving movement of the 1960s, the Hippie is the first minifigure to wear tie-dyed clothing.

Mini Facts

Likes: Anything groovy

Dislikes: Stuff that's a total drag

See Also:
Disco Dude (S2)

Bagpiper

A musician with a family history to uphold

MUSIC RUNS in the Bagpiper's blood. His father played the bagpipes, and so did his grandfather, his great-grandfather, and their fathers before them, all the way back to the day the famous instrument first arrived in Scotland. Other forms of music may come and go, but he knows that the bagpipes are forever.

New Tam o' Shanter cap element

A Secret Is Revealed

What does a Bagpiper keep under his kilt? Thanks to it being a separate fabric piece, the truth can finally be known!

New Great Highland Bagpipe piece can be held in position for playing

With his multiple tartan printings and textile kilt, the Bagpiper was one of the most complicated LEGO Minifigures to design and produce

Mini Facts

Likes: Bagpipe music

Dislikes: People who don't like bagpipe music

See Also: Highland Battler (S6)

Patterned socks

Bride

A Minifigure on her big day

THE BRIDE has been busy taking care of last-minute arrangements for her wedding. The Bagpiper is ready to play, the Rapper and Hula Dancer are set to perform, and the Galaxy Patrol is standing by in case any aliens decide to land. Now if she can just keep herself from hiccupping during the ceremony, everything will be perfect!

Mini Facts

Likes: Getting married

Dislikes: Interruptions

See Also: Waiter (S9)

Sleeveless gown

Did You Know?

A year before her release, the Bride appeared with a different face, white sleeves and a golden crown in a fan-built LEGO model to celebrate the 2011 royal wedding of Britain's Prince William and Kate Middleton.

Bouquet of pink flowers on new stem piece

Silver patterning on wedding dress

Count the spare fourth flower (included in every pack) and the Bride has the most pieces of any LEGO Minifigure

Special Occasion

Everyone loves a good wedding, but no one more so than the ever-ready Bride. All her plans have fallen into place; her tiara is sparkling, her veil is on—all she needs now is her groom!

IF YOU'RE LOOKING FOR A GROOM, I DO HAPPEN TO BE WEARING A TUXEDO!

On Stage

WHAT KIND OF PLAY IS THIS? There are historical characters, monsters, and a fairy—not to mention a couple of other eager Minifigures waiting in the wings. Whatever these wacky characters are going to perform, it looks like it is another sell-out show.

WOOAAAHHH!

MY ADORING FANS! THEY ALL LOVE ME.

Ocean King

A mighty ruler of the deep blue sea

THE OCEAN KING rules over the water from his kingdom under the sea. Powerful and temperamental, he can use his magical trident to punish litterers with sudden storms. He calms the waves for those who please him with the gift of a cookie dropped in just the right tide pool!

Mini Facts

Likes: Pizza (no anchovies)

Dislikes: Ocean polluters

See Also: Diver (S8), Mermaid (S9)

Golden trident from LEGO® Atlantis theme

New hair piece with painted crown of shells

Fish tail replaces standard minifigure legs and can attach to LEGO brick studs

Don't Mess With The King

Under his beard (originally created for the LEGO® Ninjago theme), the Ocean King's expression is just as stormy as his temper.

Did You Know?

There have been LEGO mermaids, but the Ocean King is the first-ever male mer-person minifigure.

Swimming Champion

A winner who creates her own competitions

WHEN YOU'VE already won every swimming medal, what do you do next? Not content to rest on her victories, the Swimming Champion has started making up her own extreme aquatic challenges to test her skill and endurance. From North Pole iceberg-pushing to Antarctic penguin-racing, she is determined to take the gold in every one!

New swim cap has sculpted wrinkles for a realistic look

Goggles for clear vision under water

New gold medal has a red ribbon that fits snugly around her neck

Mini Facts

Likes: The briny taste of victory

Dislikes: Water in her goggles

See Also: Deep Sea Diver (S1), Lifeguard (S2)

I CHALLENGE YOU TO HELP ME FIND THE PARTY!

Her Biggest Fan

The Swimming Champion's alternate face, free of her goggles, looks pretty pleased with her latest results. Some people say that she must be part fish, but the Ocean King swears she isn't—though he is still her number one fan!

Evil Knight

An infamous henchman-for-hire

THE EVIL KNIGHT has been a henchman for all of the big villains, from Basil the Bat Lord to Cedric the Bull. Most bad guys want wealth or power, but he just likes causing trouble and breaking stuff. He has fought in so many evil armies over the years that he sometimes forgets who he is currently working for!

Villainous Visage

The Evil Knight once spent a memorable summer as a mystical Shadow Knight. He was thrilled that he got to keep his glowing red eyes afterwards!

Boar's head symbol on shield

Dark longsword

Did You Know?

The Evil Knight's bio has references to two classic LEGO® Castle themes: 1997's Fright Knights, and the first Knights' Kingdom series from 2000.

Black armor with spiky silver details

Mini Facts

Likes: Looting and pillaging

Dislikes: Unemployment

See Also: Evil Dwarf (S5), Heroic Knight (S9)

Grandma Visitor

A little girl on a mission

THE SWEET little Grandma Visitor is skipping through the woods to her dear old granny's house. She sure hopes she won't run into any mean forest bandits…or nasty ogres…or giant spiders…or wicked wolves. Goodness, is that rain she hears up ahead? Maybe she will come back tomorrow—and bring a few friends along for backup!

Did You Know?

The Grandma Visitor is the first female character with short legs in the LEGO Minifigures line. With her basket and red hood, you don't need three guesses to see what fairy-tale character she resembles!

Who's Afraid?

The Grandma Visitor has nothing to fear from the Werewolf. He's just a big friendly puppy at heart!

Extra-large eyes, freckles, and a sweet smile help create a child minifigure's face

A short cape to match short legs

Mini Facts

Likes: Baked goods

Dislikes: Spooky noises

See Also: Leprechaun (S6), Fairy (S8)

Rubbery basket is also used in LEGO® Friends theme

WHY DOESN'T ANYBODY BRING BASKETS OF TREATS TO GRANDPAS?

Jungle Boy

A wild man who wouldn't mind some civilization

BEING RAISED by a family of chimpanzees has been pretty neat, but the Jungle Boy is getting a little tired of eating bugs and sleeping in trees, plus he keeps hearing about these things called video games.
They sure sound like a lot more fun than swinging around on vines and getting chased by leopards.

Hair piece was first used in LEGO® Prince of Persia™ sets

Necklace and scars are trophies of past adventures

Classic minifigure knife

Printed loincloth

Minifigure Pets

Animal pets and sidekicks are some of the most popular accessories in the LEGO Minifigures line, especially ones that can't be found in any other LEGO sets. They're like getting a whole extra character in your bag!

The Jungle Boy's adopted little brother

Mini Facts

Likes: Talking to animals

Dislikes: Fleeing from animals

See Also: Hockey Player (S4), Zookeeper (S5)

> I SAY, I THINK I'VE DISCOVERED A NEW SPECIES!

Computer Programmer

A Minifigure who knows his mouse from his modem

HE MAY SEEM SHY and unassuming, but the Computer Programmer is a genius with anything electronic. He knows computers inside and out, from the oldest giant mainframes to the tiniest next-generation prototypes. In just seconds, he can debug a server, wipe out a virus, and even help you set up your email if you ask nicely!

Broken glasses repaired with tape

Comfortable argyle sweater vest

Reference to an early computer interface

Mini Facts

Likes: Databases

Dislikes: Spam messages

See Also: Librarian (S10)

Secret Admirer

The Computer Programmer comes with a state-of-the-art laptop and a huge crush on the Librarian.

Opening laptop accessory first appeared in the 2008 LEGO® Agents theme

141

Tennis Ace

A prodigy with unexpected natural talent

SOME MINIFIGURES work hard all their lives to be good at their sport… and then there is the Tennis Ace. He lunges around the court with reckless abandon, swinging his racket wildly at the ball. He has no discipline, no training, and no coordination when playing. And yet somehow, he just keeps winning!

Face tense with concentration

Exclusive navy blue tennis racket

Did You Know?

The Sleepyhead's messy hair piece was a perfect match for the Tennis Ace's energetic playing style.

Matching tennis shirt and shorts

Mini Facts

Likes: Adrenaline

Dislikes: People who say he is just lucky

See Also: Tennis Player (S3)

The Ultimate Showdown

What happens when two tennis players who never lose go head-to-head? Until someone invents a LEGO tennis ball, the world may never know!

Viking Woman

A singer whose voice is as strong as her sword-arm

IF HER VILLAGE
is threatened, the Viking Woman takes up her sword and shield to fight, but it is after the battle that her talent truly shines. That is when she adds the latest verse to the village's ballad, singing it out so that all can hear and remember the great deeds of the day.

Hair and helmet (with removable horns) are a single new piece

Braids keep long hair out of the way during battle

Battle Song
The Viking Woman's two face prints were designed so that she could be used as either a mighty Viking warrior or as a classic opera singer.

Glass beads strung between shoulder-strap brooches

Did You Know?
This is the first female Viking to feature across the whole minifigure line.

143

Series 8

AUGUST 2012 Series 8 was full of new characters that complemented others, from additions to the growing music, underwater, sports, and Wild West collections to creatures straight out of the LEGO® Monster Fighters and LEGO® Alien Conquest themes!

GO, GO SERIES 8!

Businessman

Football Player

Red Cheerleader

Alien Villiane.

Cowgirl

DJ

Vampire Bat

Diver

Conquistador

Evil Robot

Lederhosen Guy

Fairy

HO HO HO!

Pirate Captain

Downhill Skier

Santa

Thespian

Thespian

A master actor who can bring any role to life

THE THESPIAN plays every role to perfection, from Romeo to Juliet (the lead actress was ill, and the show must go on). He has received many offers to appear in big-budget movies, but he always turns them down, declaring that his heart will forever belong to the stage. Besides, he would much rather direct.

Skull for reenacting scenes from the famous play "Bricklet"

16th-century-style ruff

Did You Know?

The Thespian's classic hair piece first appeared in a LEGO® set in 1983. Twenty-nine years later, his collar ruff was created by the very same LEGO designer.

Acting!

The Thespian has a very different expression on the other side of his head to demonstrate his superb acting skills.

Elizabethan-era jacket called a "doublet"

I WONDER IF THERE WILL BE A PLAY AT THE PARTY?

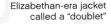

Mini Facts

Likes: Comedy, drama, tragedy

Dislikes: Reality shows

See Also: Hollywood Starlet (S9)

Conquistador

A world traveler who seeks golden riches

THE CONQUISTADOR is extremely fond of gold. He would like everything he owns to be made of it. He has traversed the globe in search of more, but for some reason, everybody he meets wants to keep theirs. He thinks it is really quite selfish that they won't share, or give it all to him!

Morion helmet with removable plume

Helmet and armor are tan plastic covered with shiny gold paint for a metallic effect

Decorated plate armor

Printed hip armor over puffy pantaloons

Gold Fever

The Conquistador is really excited—the LEGO® Minifigures line is full of unique gold-colored items and accessories!

Did You Know?

The Conquistador's helmet was originally created for the LEGO® Pirates theme in 1996. This was the first time it was produced in a color other than black.

Mini Facts

Likes:
Gold, more gold

Dislikes:
Anything not gold

See Also: Rapper (S3), Aztec Warrior (S7)

Pirate Captain

A ship-stealing seaman who just wants to be feared

THE PIRATE CAPTAIN longs to be known as the most fearsome pirate ever to sail the Seven Seas. Instead, he is mostly known for sinking every ship he has ever set foot on, for getting seasick at the sight of water, and for being unable to come up with a piratey name for himself.

Pirate's hat with golden skull and crossbones

First time this cutlass has been made in gold plastic

Wooden peg leg

Hook can h accessor just lik minifig ha

Shipmates

The Pirate Captain and the Space Villain have a lot in common, except that the Space Villain got his scars during acts of space villainy, and the Pirate Captain mostly got his in household accidents.

Did You Know?

The 1989 LEGO® Pirates theme was the first range to feature minifigures with faces with more detail than just two dots for eyes and a smile.

Mini Facts

Likes: An infamous reputation

Dislikes: Not having one

See Also: Sailor (S4), Sea Captain (S10)

Diver

A bold explorer of the ocean depths

IF HE COULD, the Diver would spend all of his life beneath the sea. He loves exploring deep-ocean trenches and shipwrecks in search of new frontiers and the answers to old mysteries. The only reason he ever returns to the surface is if someone on the ship up above forgets to pump air into his helmet.

Antique diving helmet with transparent window

Harpoon gun is only for self-defense

Mini Facts

Likes: Strolls on the ocean floor

Dislikes: Being dry

See Also: Deep Sea Diver (S1), Ocean King (S7)

Royal Pet-sitter

The Diver is good friends with the Ocean King. He sometimes asks the Diver to look after the royal pet, a catfish, when he goes out of town.

Did You Know?

The Diver's helmet uses the same lens as the magnifying glass accessory (see Explorer, S2), making his entire face look bigger.

Weighted belt and 1x1 LEGO plates on feet allow the Diver to walk around on the sea bed

Football Player

A quarterback who prepares for every game

THE FOOTBALL PLAYER practices for every possibility on the football field. He trains in snowshoes in case of blizzards. He trains in scuba gear in case of floods. He trains in math, physics, and history, just to be on the safe side. It might seem a bit much, but he knows that he'll be ready for anything!

Black grease under eyes to reduce glare from sunlight and stadium lights

Did You Know?

The LEGO Minifigures design lead chose the number 12 for the Football Player's jersey because it is the number of the quarterback who plays for her hometown team.

Mini Facts

Likes: Being prepared

Dislikes: Leaving his helmet at home

See Also: Baseball Player (S3), Soccer Player (S4)

Separated At Sports

With different colors and decorations, the Hockey Player's padding and helmet are the perfect fit for an American football player's gear.

Number printed on front and back of jersey

New trophy cup element

Red Cheerleader

A leader who won't be out-cheered

THE RED CHEERLEADER is all about outdoing the competition. If another cheering squad creates a human pyramid, then she leads her squad in forming a human sphinx. If the other team's halftime show has fireworks, she gets a skywriter jet. More fans come to watch the cheering than the game!

Long black hair pulled up in a high ponytail

Same enthusiasm as the Cheerleader, but louder

Did You Know?

The Series 1 Cheerleader's "M" stands for VP Matthew Ashton's first initial. The "A" on the Red Cheerleader stands for his last.

Same pom-poms as the Cheerleader, but with red tips

Friendly Rivals

The Red Cheerleader doesn't have anything against her blue-shirted rival. She just thinks the best cheers lead to the best wins—and she wants her team to be the best!

Mini Facts

Likes: Putting on the best show

Dislikes: Being outdone

See Also: Cheerleader (S1)

Lederhosen Guy

A Minifigure who really loves his lederhosen

THE LEDERHOSEN GUY is very proud of his fine leather shorts. He goes to lederhosen conventions, posts on lederhosen forums, and even writes his own lederhosen blog. That's how he came to be known as the Lederhosen Guy, instead of just a guy who wears lederhosen!

A new color for a classic cap

It's A Great Big Mini World

Some Minifigures are designed to represent a particular fashion or tradition from around the world. Builders can use them to add an international flair to their LEGO models.

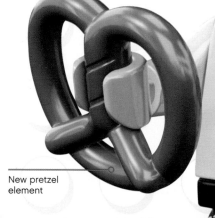

Lederhosen were originally worn as work clothes, but have become a Bavarian cultural institution

New pretzel element

Did You Know?

Having made a lot of characters based on American icons, the LEGO Minifigures' designers wanted to give a shout-out to their European fans—thus the Bavarian-style Lederhosen Guy!

Mini Facts

Likes: Lederhosen

Dislikes: Long pants

See Also: Highland Battler (S6), Bagpiper (S7)

Santa

A legendary donator of bricks

ACCORDING TO THE STORIES, the mysterious Santa flies through the sky on his sleigh, giving out shiny new bricks to anybody who needs to get some building done. But where do all of those bricks come from, and what is Santa's secret connection to the LEGO factory in Denmark? Whatever the answers may be, he is not telling.

New hat element is white plastic decorated with glossy red paint

Close Shave

Without his famous white beard, you can barely recognize jolly old Santa.

The Fisherman's beard is just right for Santa's whiskers

Did You Know?

This isn't the first Santa Claus minifigure, but he is the very first one to have his own newly designed hat and sack of presents.

New sack accessory can be held or attached to LEGO bricks.

Mini Facts

Likes: Nice people

Dislikes: Naughty people

See Also: Leprechaun (S6), Fairy (S8)

MAKE PRESENTS? SORRY, BUT I'M NOT THAT KIND OF ELF.

153

Playing Sports

THE MINIFIGURES like to keep in shape with plenty of fresh air and exercise. That is why they have built themselves a giant park with skating ramps, ski slopes, a swimming pool, tracks, and fields for practicing different sports.

STILL NO WAVES? HEY, SPLASH AROUND A LITTLE MORE IN THERE!

GO RED!

WOOO! CHECK OUT WHAT I JUST WON!

THAT'S NOT A TROPHY. THIS IS A TROPHY!

NO WAY! GO BLUE!

Octan

Fairy

A magical sprite who is kind of mixed-up

THE FAIRY spends so much time flitting to and fro that she frequently forgets what kind of fairy she is supposed to be. Does she turn rocks into handsome princes? Should she leave glass slippers under pillows? Fortunately, no matter how confused she gets, a wave of her magic wand creates a happy ending.

Enchanted flower mark on cheek

Transparent-pink wand

Series 8 is the first LEGO Minifigures series to feature characters with wings

Did You Know?

The Fairy's magic wand is a LEGO piece that first appeared in 1993. It has made appearances in themes including LEGO® Castle, BELVILLE™, Time Cruisers, and Harry Potter™.

New leaf-shaped fabric skirt

Mini Facts

Likes: Sleeping in flowers

Dislikes: Angry bees

See Also: Genie (S6), Bumblebee Girl (S10)

EXCUSE ME, MISS FAIRY? OH, I DON'T THINK SHE CAN HEAR ME OVER HER WINGS...

Flights Of Fancy

The Fairy's translucent blue wings are a new element that attaches via a bracket around her neck. Unlike the Clockwork Robot's key, the wings and bracket are all one piece.

Vampire Bat

A creature of darkness who favors the light

BY NIGHT he is the chief hench-bat in the castle of a wicked monster lord, but at dawn, the Vampire Bat likes to sneak out to enjoy the daytime. His master may scheme to blot out the sun, but he would much rather frolic and soar in the light—even if it is a little hard to see when it is so bright outside!

Hair piece with big ears for echolocation

Dark fur detailing

Arms rotate at the shoulder and wrist

The Vampire Bat is a cousin to the brown man-bats from LEGO® Monster Fighters

Special Sculpts

Most minifigures share the same basic body parts, but a few feature special parts, such as the Vampire Bat's wings or the Mermaid's tail that gives them a unique look, pose, or function.

Did You Know?

The Vampire Bat's boss is Lord Vampyre from the LEGO® Monster Fighters theme—not to be confused with the much nicer Vampire from LEGO® Minifigures Series 1.

Mini Facts

Likes: Sand castles and songbirds

Dislikes: Darkness and gloom

See Also: Vampire (S2), Werewolf (S4)

Cowgirl

A lasso-slinger from the Wild West

NOBODY IS QUICKER with a lasso than the high-spirited Cowgirl. Whether she is pulling a calf out of a ravine, stopping a stampeding bison in its tracks, or rounding up a stage-robbing outlaw, she can throw her rope quicker than the eye can follow. She always catches whatever she happens to be aiming at, too!

Mini Facts

Likes: The Cowboy

Dislikes: No-good varmints

See Also: Cowboy (S1), Bandit (S6)

White Western hat with painted braid in back

Freckles

Made of soft plastic, the lasso can fit around a minifigure to capture it

Rodeo wear

The Big Round-Up

The Cowgirl's lasso piece was first used as Wonder Woman's Golden Lasso of Truth in the LEGO® DC Universe™ Super Heroes theme.

Did You Know?

Many modern LEGO elements are designed on computers, but the Cowgirl's new hat-and-hair piece was sculpted by hand.

Cowboy (or is that cowgirl?) boots

Downhill Skier

A Minifigure who always thinks things are looking up

THE ETERNALLY OPTIMISTIC

Downhill Skier believes that life is like a snow-covered mountain. There may be twists and turns along the way, and hidden obstacles lurking beneath the snow, but as long as you tuck in and keep your eyes on your destination, you are sure to reach your goal at top speed.

When you ski this fast, you don't need a hat to keep you warm

Bright colors make skiers easier to see against the snow

A vivid new look for skis owned by the Series 2 Skier

Blazing Speed

A pro at the fastest of all alpine-skiing disciplines, the Downhill Skier has learnt how to position her body to achieve maximum velocity as she slides down the slopes.

Did You Know?

The Downhill Skier features some of the new plastic colors that were introduced in the 2012 LEGO® Friends theme.

Mini Facts

Likes: The bright side

Dislikes: Negativity

See Also: Skier (S2), Snowboarder Guy (S5)

Evil Robot

An evil opposite built to destroy

THE EVIL ROBOT was programmed to be the Robot's exact opposite. If the Robot finds bricks to build towers, then the Evil Robot smashes models and hides the pieces. The Robot walks forwards, so the Evil Robot runs backwards. The Robot is a hard worker, so the Evil Robot is totally lazy. It isn't the most useful evil minion.

Glaring red eyes are often closed for naps

Beneath The Bucket

Despite its odd behavior, villains keep recruiting the Evil Robot to help with their schemes. They usually figure out pretty quickly that having an evil opposite on your side isn't as handy as it sounds.

Did You Know?

Due to the rarity of the Series 1 Robot, the Evil Robot was created as both a substitute for new fans and a fun counterpart for collectors who owned the original.

Laser gun fires harmless beam of light

Claw arm is surprisingly slow at destruction

Mini Facts

Likes: Dismantling

Dislikes: Being shiny and clean

See Also: Bandit (S6), Evil Knight (S7)

Alien Villainess

An extraterrestrial empress bent on universal conquest

WITH A NAME far too regal (and long and unpronounceable) to speak out loud, the Alien Villainess rules over a vast interstellar empire. From her throne-world citadel, she sends out fleets of flying saucers to every corner of the galaxy with orders to conquer any planets they find.

NO MATTER WHAT YOU TRY, YOUR MAJESTY, I WILL DEFEAT YOU!

Pink brain constantly hatches evil plots

New two-piece cape and collar

Mini Facts

Likes: Absolute control of outer space

Dislikes: Intergalactic Girl

See Also: Space Alien (S3), Space Villain (S3)

Astro Foes

The Alien Villainess is the empress of the invaders from the 2011 LEGO® Alien Conquest theme. Her evil plots to control space are constantly thwarted by the heroine Intergalactic Girl from Series 6.

Symbol of the Alien Conquest armada

Disintegrator ray blaster

Belt with flying saucer logo

Imperial robes conceal tentacles

Did You Know?

The Alien Villainess is the first official female rogue in the LEGO Minifigures line.

DJ

A music lover who shares his knowledge

THE DJ is the number one disc jockey in town. Call in with a request for any song, band, or style of music and he won't just play it, but he will tell you all about its history, too. Being a walking encyclopedia of facts is not something he has trained for. He just loves music that much.

New hair piece is the first to have sculpted-on headphones

Did You Know?

The names on the DJ's record album are inspired by two LEGO designers who also DJ. "Hollywood Dawes" is Laurence Dawes, and "DJ Rhusty" is Andy Coghill.

Mini Facts

Likes: All types of music

Dislikes: People who hate the classics

See Also: Disco Dude (S2), Rocker Girl (S7)

T-shirt design with audio output in the shape of a minifigure head

The DJ's favorite chart-topping album

I'M OFF TO BOOGIE!

WAIT! LET ME TELL YOU SOME MORE.

Music Mania

The DJ loves taking song requests. Just don't expect to hear them played too soon—he will give you a detailed history of the song before he plays it.

Businessman

An entirely ordinary fellow

THE BUSINESSMAN is a completely normal office worker, and not in any way a highly trained secret agent who goes on daring undercover missions all over the world. He puts in a standard day's work, earning a standard wage at a standard place of business. Don't believe anything else you hear.

Bowler hat does not have built-in listening gear or a grappling line

Read All About It!

Just like the DJ's album cover, the Businessman's newspaper is printed on a 2x2 LEGO tile. It certainly looks like a regular edition of a daily newspaper....

Plain black business suit is not filled with hi-tech espionage gadgets

Did You Know?

There are a lot of British designers on the LEGO Minifigures team, so the Businessman was patterned after an old-fashioned Englishman in an old-fashioned bowler hat.

Mini Facts

Likes: Reading about finances

Dislikes: Foiling super-villain plots

See Also: Royal Guard (S5)

Briefcase does not contain classified secrets

Newspaper is not well-camouflaged datapad with a remote satellite uplink

EVEN I CAN DETECT NOTHING OUT OF THE ORDINARY HERE!

63

Series 9

JANUARY 2013 From a rubber plunger to a knightly sword, and from a battle mech's helmet to a judge's wig, Series 9 was loaded with new elements to expand the world of LEGO® building. Oh, and let's not forget the chicken wings.

Hollywood Starlet

Mr. Good and Evil

I REALLY LIKE IT HERE! NO, I HATE IT...I LIKE IT! NO...

Heroic Knight

Judge

I JUDGE THIS TO BE THE BES[T] SERIES!

Waiter

Roller Derby Girl

Roman Emperor

Cyclops

Forest Maiden

Plumber

Fortune Teller

OFF TO SAVE THE DAY! AGAIN!

Battle Mech

Policeman

Chicken Suit Guy

Alien Avenger

Mermaid

Heroic Knight

A noble hero in shining armor

THE HEROIC KNIGHT is the greatest hero of his age. He rides across the land, fighting for justice and righting wrongs wherever he finds them. He sometimes gets things a little bit backwards—like when he rescued that dragon from a princess—but he is just so valiant that everybody cheers for him anyway.

Sword, shield, and removable breastplate are molded in shiny silver

Printed filigree and armor details

Did You Know?

The Heroic Knight's visor, shield, and armor are classic LEGO® Castle elements. His sword, though similar to the original, is a new piece with a more detailed hilt and cross-guard.

The Champion's Helm

The Heroic Knight's pointed visor was first introduced in 1990. It can swing open and has holes for attaching plumes and other ornaments on the top and on both sides.

Mini Facts

Likes: Saving the day

Dislikes: Squeaking armor

See Also: Elf (S3), Evil Knight (S7)

Forest Maiden

An elusive mistress of the woods

THE FOREST MAIDEN knows each root and branch of the woods by heart. As a member of the Forestman's merry band, she is skilled at building traps to capture anyone who invades her forest home. Any enemy who avoids her snares quickly learns that her shield and bow aren't just for decoration.

Hair braided with strips of bark

The Forest Maiden is skilled at shooting her longbow

Mini Facts

Likes: Woodcarving

Dislikes: Trespassers

See Also: Forestman (S1)

Tree symbol represents her love for the forest

Woodland Romance

Just as the Forestman from Series 1 was based on a famous outlaw, so the Forest Maiden is inspired by his beloved maid.

Did You Know?

The Forest Maiden's new hair piece is made of soft plastic. It was designed so that it could also be used for other forest-dwelling female characters, like one from a galaxy far, far away....

167

Hollywood Starlet

A celebrated actress of the silver screen

THE HOLLYWOOD STARLET is on the fast track to becoming the most popular actress in the world. As beautiful as she is talented, she can make the audience laugh or move them to tears with a well-rehearsed word. Her fans can't wait to see what movie she will shoot next!

Top film award for her acting in "The 7-Stud Brick"

New hair piece takes three hours to style

Fabulous diamond pendant

Movie Magic

The Hollywood Starlet's greatest dream is to work with the Thespian to make the greatest motion picture of all time. She has tried everything to convince him that they must act together, but he still refuses to step in front of a camera!

Did You Know?

The Hollywood Starlet has 372 sequins printed on her dress.

Mini Facts

Likes: Challenging roles

Dislikes: Improvising

See Also: Thespian (S8)

Dress made by a leading fashion designer

Plumber

A workman who doesn't mind messy jobs

THE GOOD-HUMORED PLUMBER takes on any job with a smile, no matter how bad it may look. As long as he has got his trusty plunger and can-do attitude, there is nothing he can't handle...and that is good, because you would not believe some of the strange things he has bumped into down in the sewers.

New worker's cap element

Zip on pocket keeps plumbing tools from falling out

"Ole Plungey," the Plumber's best friend

Did You Know?

The Plumber's new plunger accessory has a hard plastic handle and a soft, rubbery cup that can really suction onto things.

Dressed For The Job

After his plunger, the Plumber's second-most-important piece of equipment is his pair of overalls. The pockets hold lots of things that have helped him get through sticky situations!

Mini Facts

Likes: Putting in a good day's work

Dislikes: Subterranean mutants

See Also: Hazmat Guy (S4)

THERE'S NO ONE I'D RATHER CALL WHEN DEALING WITH SLUDGE THAT GLOWS, OR MOVES, OR TALKS!

169

Policeman

A public servant in hot pursuit

THE BRAVE POLICEMAN may be based in the big city, but he will go anywhere to catch crooks and bring them to justice. Wherever robbers flee, they will hear his footsteps following behind them…and just when they think they've gotten away with the loot, on go the handcuffs and off they go to jail!

New realistic police cap element with painted brim and shield

Cuff 'Em!

Originally a LEGO® City element, the Policeman's soft-plastic handcuffs can be held in the middle or put around a minifigure's wrists to place them under arrest.

Uniform is detailed down to golden tie clip and pen in his pocket

Flipped-open badge is printed on a 1x2 tile, the shield in silver and the I.D. card in white

Did You Know?

The Policeman's badge number is "2101", which stands for designer Michael Patton's birthday, on the 21st of January.

Mini Facts

Likes: Catching bad guys

Dislikes: Lawbreakers

See Also: Traffic Cop (S2), Judge (S9)

Judge

A decisive force of judgment

THE STERN JUDGE has the final word on everything. When court is in session, he separates the innocent from the guilty. Outside the courtroom, he keeps on judging everything he sees, from the flowers in the garden to the condiments on his hamburger—all with a bang of his gavel.

NOT GUILTY!

PHEW!

Courtroom Dramas

The Judge always thinks hard before making a decision, and he never pounds his gavel until he is sure that he has made the right one.

New soft plastic wig makes the Judge look extra-important

New gavel is perfect for banging on objects after making judgments

Traditional British court dress including a wing collar with two formal bands

Did You Know?

The Judge's ceremonial "full-bottom" wig was sculpted at 3x its final size during the design process so that the designers could best capture the shape and details.

Red version of the Graduate's fabric robe from Series 5

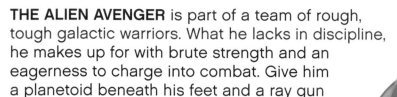

Alien Avenger

A battle-hungry space commando

THE ALIEN AVENGER is part of a team of rough, tough galactic warriors. What he lacks in discipline, he makes up for with brute strength and an eagerness to charge into combat. Give him a planetoid beneath his feet and a ray gun in his hand, and he'll take on anything you point him toward!

The Alien Avenger already has a hard head—his helmet just makes it harder

Face In A Crowd

The Alien Avenger was created as a counterpart (though not necessarily a bad guy) to the Series 7 Galaxy Patrol. As one of 5,000 identical siblings, he doesn't mind if some see him as just another nameless trooper.

Did You Know?

The word "SHAMI" printed under the Alien Avenger's armor is the nickname of LEGO designer Frédéric Andre.

Armor scavenged from the battlefields of a hundred war-torn worlds

Mini Facts

Likes: Fighting

Dislikes: Not fighting

See Also:
Galaxy Patrol (S7)

Mr. Good And Evil

A Minifigure who is in two minds about everything

WITH HIS MIND and body divided in a laboratory accident, Mr. Good and Evil's nice and not-so-nice sides are in a constant struggle. Half of him wants to help people, while the other half craves chaos and destruction. Everything good he does ends up a little bad, and everything bad comes out a little good!

19th-century, Victorian-style gentleman's clothes

Mini Facts

Likes: Good deeds/bad deeds

Dislikes: Bad deeds/good deeds

See Also: Crazy Scientist (S4)

Will this potion cure Mr. Good and Evil, or transform him even more?

A new color combination for the Crazy Scientist's flask

Inner Voices

Some people have an imaginary angel and devil to give them advice, but Mr. Good and Evil has robots. One tells him to build, the other to deconstruct!

ALWAYS NICE TO MEET ANOTHER MAD SCIENTIST! AH-HA-HA-HA!

In The City

THE STREETS are teeming with busy Minifigures just trying to get on with their day. They may have different jobs, hobbies, and destinations, but they know that it takes all kinds of Minifigures to make a city run.

Living Statue

City Financial News

Fortune Teller

A flawed predictor of the future

THE FORTUNE TELLER has a unique gift for seeing the future, but she is only right half of the time. Since she never knows whether a fortune will come true or not, she gives her customers one prediction, and then provides an opposite one! It may be confusing, but at least she knows she will always be half right.

New hair piece with painted scarf and coins

Fortune's Favor

The Fortune Teller once told the Hazmat Guy that he wouldn't have to clean up after any slimy mutants that week. She got that one very wrong indeed.

Mini Facts

Likes: Being totally right

Dislikes: Being completely wrong

See Also: Magician (S1)

Elaborately printed dress details

176

Waiter

A well-mannered facilitator of fine dining

THE WAITER is the very model of balance, manners, and poise. He knows what drink to serve with every meal, though that might be because he only has one bottle, and he serves it every time. The only things that rattle his nearly unflappable nerves (and serving tray) are unexpected noises like coughs and sneezes.

Don't tell anyone, but the Waiter's perfectly groomed hair is actually plastic

Bottle sits on tray but doesn't snap in place—hope your balance is as good as the Waiter's!

New serving tray element attaches to the top of a minifigure hand

Did You Know?

The Waiter's bottle was originally labeled "Chateau retesacque" in honor of French LEGO designer Raphaël Pretesacque, but there wasn't enough space on the label.

HONK! HONK!

Mini Facts

Likes: Giving dining recommendations

Dislikes: Bad tippers

See Also: Butcher (S6)

Well-Suited

The LEGO Minifigures line has quite a few sharply dressed characters in suits and tuxedos...and a few not-so-dapper ones, too.

Cyclops

A one-eyed guardian of the forbidden island

FOREVER WATCHFUL and alert, Cyclops guards the shores of his uncharted island home, roaring at any boat that sails too close. What nobody knows is that deep down, this ferocious-looking creature is actually a very sensitive soul. If only he could find a friend with whom he could finally see eye-to-eye.

Beneath his mask-like face, Cyclops has a printed head with two alternate expressions

Quite An Eyeful

The Sailor and Cyclops have more than a love of the sea in common—the Sailor has a permanent wink, which means he can only see out of one eye.

Gray version of the Series 1 Caveman's stone club

Armored girdle with metallic copper accents and cyclopean skull

Did You Know?

The Cyclops was produced in a new olive-green plastic color that was first introduced to LEGO sets in 2012.

Mini Facts

Likes: Making driftwood art

Dislikes: Allergy season

See Also: Minotaur (S6), Medusa (S10)

Mermaid

An ocean-dweller who wants to see the world

MOST MERMAIDS spend their time frolicking and singing, but this one wants to become the first mer-person ever to swim all the way around the world. The Mermaid is having a great time so far on her voyage, but she wishes she could find an underwater mailbox to send some postcards back home.

Kindred Swimmers

Until she ran into the Swimming Champion, the Mermaid never knew that people with legs like to swim too. It made her want to learn more about the strange surface world.

Did You Know?

The Mermaid's tail piece (which she shares with the Ocean King) was originally produced for the LEGO® Pirates of the Caribbean™ theme. It is the second LEGO mermaid tail element.

The first time this mermaid tail piece has been made in this shade of blue

Silver-printed scale pattern

Mini Facts

Likes: Taking people-spotting tours

Dislikes: Sore fins from too much swimming

See Also: Swimming Champion (S7), Ocean King (S7)

Roller Derby Girl

A wheeled warrior who is on a roll

THE ROLLER DERBY GIRL is one of the best scorers around, but once she starts speeding up on her skates, she just keeps going faster and faster. By the end of the game, she is a red-and-blue blur, leaving scorch marks in her wake. When she finally stops, she sometimes finds herself in a totally new place.

Star on helmet designates a jammer, or scoring player

Roller derby team colors

Mini Facts

Likes: Jamming

Dislikes: Anyone who gets in her way

See Also: Skater (S1)

Totally Tubular

Although the LEGO skateboard and ice skates elements can't connect to the tops of bricks, the Roller Derby Girl's new roller skates have tubes underneath so that they can attach to LEGO studs.

Elbow pads printed on arms

Did You Know?

The number 49 on the Roller Derby Girl's uniform is the team number of the designer's favorite baseball player.

Battle Mech

A futuristic planetary protector

WHENEVER THE WORLD is in danger, the mighty Battle Mech rockets into action. Launching from its secret base, it uses its built-in weaponry to battle space monsters, out-of-control asteroids, and other perils. No one knows who created the mechanized hero and controls it on its missions, but they sure are glad it is here.

No one knows if this helmet covers remote-controlled electronics or whether there's a pilot inside

Did You Know?

How do you design a helmet and armor for a futuristic warrior? If you're the LEGO® designers, you build them digitally on a computer to create new parts with perfect precision.

Japanese comic, super-robot-design style

New armor piece has similar jetpack connections on the back to the Galaxy Patrol's and Alien Avenger's armor

Mysterious Hero

The Battle Mech is a notoriously elusive character. Once it has saved the world from near destruction, it takes off, and disappears into space.

Mini Facts

Likes: Unknown

Dislikes: Unknown

See Also: Also unknown

WOW! NOW THAT'S ONE HI-TECH TOY!

181

Chicken Suit Guy

A guy in a chicken suit

THE CHICKEN SUIT GUY started out as a fast-food mascot, but he knew that he could be so much more. Now he roams the world in search of people who need his help. If you are looking for someone to dance around, flap his arms, and make clucking noises—you know who to call.

Feathered Hero

Can dressing up like poultry really help you save the day? Just ask the grateful citizens of the LEGO world and they will tell you how glad they are to have a guy in a chicken suit on their side!

Chicken mask was hand-sculpted by the LEGO Minifigures design team

Did You Know?

Thanks to his identical wings and his plain white chest, the Chicken Suit Guy is the first minifigure (not counting classic LEGO skeletons) to have a torso that looks exactly the same from the front and the back.

YOU MUST BE A FELLOW WARRIOR OF THE SUN...I'VE HEARD YOU CROW TO WELCOME THE DAY!

Mini Facts

Likes: Going wherever he is needed most

Dislikes: Disrespect for the chicken suit

See Also: Gorilla Suit Guy (S3), Bunny Suit Guy (S7)

Printed claws on feet

Roman Emperor

A leader who is used to getting what he wants

THE ROMAN EMPEROR is accustomed to getting his way all the time. He expects the other Minifigures to polish his sandals, feed him grapes, and carry him around wherever he wants to go. His favorite thing to do is make up new rules for everybody to follow, like naming months after his favorite food and pets.

Did You Know?

The text "Veni, Vidi, Vici" printed on the Roman Emperor's 2x2 tile is Latin for "I came, I saw, I conquered"—a famous quote said to have been written by Julius Caesar.

A Royal Pain

Ever since he met the Egyptian Queen at one of the Vampire's parties, the Roman Emperor has been trying to get her to pay attention to him. If only he knew that she would never be willing to share her throne!

New hair piece with golden leaf crown

VENI,
VIDI, VICI

Gold embroidery is reserved for generals and emperors

Toga draped around body

Mini Facts

Likes: The month of Hamstertober

Dislikes: Disobedient Minifigures

See Also: Roman Soldier (S6), Roman Commander (S10)

Series 10

MAY 2013 How do you celebrate ten awesome series of LEGO® Minifigures? With golden packaging, even more new characters and parts, and for the first time, a harder-to-find 17th figure: the mysterious and lucky Mr. Gold!

Sea Captain

Decorator

Warrior Woman

Librarian

SHHHH!

IN MY DAY, MINIFIGURES WERE HEARD AND NOT SEEN!

Oranges and Peaches

Shhh!

Grandpa

Tomahawk Warrior

Paintballer

Roman Commander

Warrior Woman

A savage fighter with a secret past

THE WARRIOR WOMAN has earned her fame in pitched battle with pirates and brigands all across the land. Her fierce and uncivilized manner hides a secret: she was raised as the princess of a distant kingdom, but grew tired of the royal life and ran off to be a mighty warrior instead.

Did You Know?

Unlike the Gladiator, Roman Soldier, and similar characters, the Warrior Woman's design isn't based on a specific historical period. Instead, she's inspired by the style of barbarian-fantasy books and movies.

Long spear keeps enemies at a distance

Mini Facts

Likes: Weapons and armor

Dislikes: Crowns and finery

See Also: Spartan Warrior (S2), Gladiator (S5)

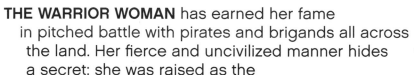

Royal Renegade

The Warrior Woman has never regretted her decision to give up her throne in favor of defending the weak and helpless—but her opponents often do!

The Warrior Woman's eagle symbol is known wherever she travels

Librarian

A lifelong lover of books and reading

READING IS THE LIBRARIAN'S most cherished pastime. No matter where she is, she can always sit down with a good book and travel to far-off lands, meet new friends, and discover exciting stories and cultures. If only everybody loved books as much as she does, the world would be a better place...and much quieter, too!

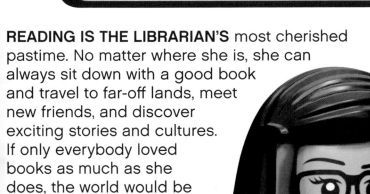

This is the expression you'll receive if you don't respect books properly

The Librarian knitted this sleeveless sweater herself

Silence Is Golden

Even the Maraca Man knows to keep the volume low when the Librarian is taking care of her books. If he's especially quiet, she might read him a story!

Her mug has a message for anybody who makes too much noise in the library

Did You Know?

The "Oranges and Peaches" book title comes from a library joke about a mishearing of "On the Origin of Species" by Charles Darwin.

Oranges and Peaches

IT SURE IS QUIET. I GUESS THERE'S NO PARTY GOING ON HERE.

Sad Clown

An inconsolable tragedian

TO THE SAD CLOWN, everything is a tragedy. Things that make other people smile and laugh only fill him with sadness and woe. The other Minifigures try to cheer him up, but it just makes him even more sad. They don't understand that he's only truly happy when he is completely miserable.

New cone-shaped hat

Black version of the Thespian's collar

The Sad Clown is the second black-and-white Minifigure

Did You Know?

The Sad Clown was inspired by Pierrot, a pantomime character dating back to an Italian performance in late 17th-century France.

No smiles on this clown's face, only melancholy

Mini Facts

Likes: Sitting, sighing

Dislikes: Knock-knock jokes

See Also: Circus Clown (S1), Mime (S2)

Happy vs. Sad

Not even puppies, kittens, and funny videos can turn the Sad Clown's frown upside-down. Some say that the Circus Clown got him to giggle once, but the Sad Clown insists it was just a sniffle.

Decorator

A Minifigure with a colorful job

THE DECORATOR doesn't just paint houses. It is his very important job to add a color to each new LEGO® brick as it rolls off the assembly line. You didn't think they just popped out of a big machine like that, did you? No, it is all down to this fellow and his little paint roller!

At The Factory

It's a tough job, making sure that every LEGO brick has an even coat of color, right down to the hollow tubes underneath. But the Decorator is just the Minifigure to do it!

White version of the Series 9 Plumber's hat

Overalls keep clothes underneath clean

Mini Facts

Likes: Adding special decorations

Dislikes: Mismatched purples

See Also: Artist (S4)

Did You Know?

The round LEGO piece on the Decorator's paint roller can be replaced with other colors to represent whatever shade he's painting at the moment.

ALAS, I HAVE PAINTED SUNRISES, FLOWERS, AND LANDSCAPES...BUT NEVER HAVE I HAD THE CHANCE TO PAINT BRICKS!

189

Skydiver

A parachutist about to make his first jump

THE SKYDIVER has trained so hard for this very moment. Now all he has to do is get the courage to hop out of an airplane flying thousands of feet above the ground. His helmet is in place, his straps and buckles are secure, and his parachute is on his back. It is time to hold his breath, close his eyes, and go!

High-visibility helmet and backpack in case he drifts off course

Mouth rippling from speed of fall, or is that just nerves?

Ripcord deploys parachute for a controlled drop

Taking The Plunge

A new parachute pack element was created for the Skydiver to ensure a safe landing on the ground far below.

Mini Facts

Likes: Landing

Dislikes: Falling

See Also: Pilot (S3)

Baseball Fielder

An outfielder with a talent for amazing catches

WITH THE HELP of his leather mitt, the Baseball Fielder can catch just about any object that is hurled into the air. Over the course of his career, he has caught everything from line drives and pop flies to souvenirs dropped by fans—not to mention a runaway rocket and a falling star or two.

Team logo on baseball cap

Major League

It may have taken two years, but with the Baseball Fielder's release in LEGO Minifigures Series 10, the Baseball Player finally has someone to play against!

Mini Facts

Likes: Catching baseballs

Dislikes: Catching colds

See Also: Baseball Player (S4)

Did You Know?

The Baseball Fielder's team is called the Stackers, which refers to the process of stacking LEGO bricks together.

New baseball mitt element replaces the standard minifigure hand

Two-toned baseball uniform

191

Grandpa

A grumbler who doesn't like anything new

GRANDPA PREFERRED EVERYTHING the way it used to be, and he will tell you so every chance he gets. He does not like all of these new-fangled electronic gadgets and reality TV shows. He doesn't like the internet or microwave pizza. He doesn't even like any LEGO piece that isn't a good old-fashioned brick.

That comb-over isn't fooling anybody

Old Fashioned

Grandpa has a unique look. The Rapper and the Punk Rocker think he's really trendy! Little do they know, his clothes are more for comfort than style.

Printed top of hiked-up pants

Bow ties never go out of fashion

Did You Know

Grandpa would be grumpy if he knew that he has a brand-new hair piece—the first minifigure bald cap!

Grandpa gets all of his news from this 1900s vintage newspaper

Mini Facts

Likes: Old stuff

Dislikes: Anything invented after 1910.

See Also: Caveman (S1)

OLD TIMES

I REMEMBER THIS GUY BEING OLD BACK WHEN I WAS A KID!

Trendsetter

A social celebrity who leads the way

WHATEVER THE TRENDSETTER does becomes the next big thing. Everybody she meets wants to look like her, act like her, and do everything she likes to do. Unfortunately for her, that means that her favorite clothes, ice cream flavors, and movies are always sold out, but aside from that, she thinks all the attention is awesome.

New hair piece is all the rage

Fashion Clones

In the Minifigures' world, if you want your hair and clothes to look exactly like someone else's, all you have to do is borrow them!

Mini Facts

Likes: Being popular

Dislikes: Being ignored

See Also: Pop Star (S2), Rapper (S3)

New Chihuahua is the year's most popular dog breed

Extremely trendy bling

The hottest smartphone, fashionably printed on a 1x2 tile

Did You Know?

While this is not the first LEGO dog, the Trendsetter's pet Chihuahua is certainly the smallest.

Roman Commander

A general who is expecting victory

THE ROMAN COMMANDER is looking forward to leading the legions of Rome to triumph and glory. He has studied all the greatest historical battles and is certain that his knowledge of tactics will win the day. He sometimes worries about only having one soldier in his army, but at least it makes it easy to shout commands.

New horsehair crest plugs into the top of the helmet that first appeared with the Roman Soldier

Wolf symb represent the adopt mother of Romulu the mythi founder of Rome

Armored breastplate of a high-ranking Roman

Classic Hierarchy

The Roman Emperor gives orders to the Roman Commander, and the Roman Commander gives them to the Roman Soldier.

Did You Know?

When the Roman Soldier was released in Series 6, fans requested an officer to command him. They finally got their wish in Series 10.

Mini Facts

Likes:
Giving orders

Dislikes:
Surrendering

See Also: Roman Soldier (S6), Roman Emperor (S9)

Bumblebee Girl

A busy girl who is all abuzz about honey

THE BUMBLEBEE GIRL loves honey so much that she decided to dress up and join a hive. She buzzes around the meadow all day, gathering nectar and pollen with her new bee friends. It turns out that bumblebees don't really make much honey, but she is having too much fun to stop.

New antenna-cap element

The first time the pot accessory has had printing

Minifigure Menagerie

Here comes a parade of Minifigures in silly animal suits! You won't find figures like these in any other LEGO theme.

Rosy cheeks as a result of lots of fresh air

Colorless-version of the Series 8 Fairy's wings

Mini Facts

Likes: Flowers and honey

Dislikes: Hungry bears

See Also: Bunny Suit Guy (S7), Chicken Suit Guy (S9)

Did You Know?

The Bumblebee Girl is the first female costumed LEGO Minifigures character.

195

Revolutionary Soldier
A patriot who fights for the freedom of all Minifigures

THE REVOLUTIONARY SOLDIER'S greatest wish is to see all Minifigures across the land be free of oppression and tyranny. He doesn't like to fight, but he will do whatever he can to help make his dream a reality. He knows he is here to stand up for independence and the rights of the little guy.

White cross-belts for holding equipment

Historical Hairdo

The Revolutionary Soldier's new hair piece is based on the powdered wigs worn during the American Revolutionary War of the late 18th century.

Uniform of the American Continental Army

Blue soldier's coat with red trimmings

Mini Facts

Likes: Freedom and equality

Dislikes: Tea

See Also: Lady Liberty (S6)

I JUDGE YOUR WIG TO BE ALMOST AS EXCELLENT AS MINE!

Did You Know?

The Revolutionary Soldier's musket first appeared in the LEGO® Pirates theme in 1989.

Motorcycle Mechanic

A repairman who doesn't mind clanks and rattles

WANT YOUR RIDE to roar? Just take it to the Motorcycle Mechanic. He may look scruffy, but he knows motorcycles inside and out. Your bike won't look pretty by the time he is done banging on it with his wrench, but it will definitely run faster, further, and noisier than it ever did before.

Sleeveless denim jacket

Skull-and-wrench belt buckle

An oil-stained rag is the only cleaning equipment he needs

The Minifigure world's first printed flame tattoo

Spanner In The Works?

When it comes to the nuts and bolts of a problem, you can always rely on the Motorcycle Mechanic and the Mechanic to get the job done.

Did You Know?

Until the Series 8 Santa was released, the Motorcycle Mechanic's red bandana (originally from the LEGO® Pirates range) had always been used as the hat for Santa Claus minifigures.

Sea Captain

A man of the sea who has seen it all

THE SEA CAPTAIN has been a nautical man for so long, he can't count how many times he has run into raging whirlpools, mysterious island paradises, and ravenous krakens. It all used to be really exciting, but nowadays when something extraordinary happens, he just yawns and double-checks his course.

New peaked cap element

Seagull can perch on the Sea Captain's hand (or head)

Did You Know?

Although brick-built LEGO® seagulls existed before the Sea Captain, this is the first one to be made from a single piece.

Printed rank stripes with executive curl

Spotting danger early is the best way to avoid it

Mini Facts

Likes: Clear skies and calm waves

Dislikes: Distractions

See Also: Sailor (S4), Pirate Captain (S8)

All Hands On Deck

Some captains might consider seagulls to be pests, but the Sea Captain has liked them ever since one helped him find his way back to port in a storm.

Medusa

A mythological menace with a petrifying gaze

MEDUSA HAS THE POWER to turn anyone that looks directly at her into solid stone. Some might see this as a curse, but she thinks it is tremendous fun, and is always disappointed when the effect wears off a few hours later. She loves to hide and then jump out to scare unsuspecting Minifigures stiff!

Eyes are normally green, but turn orange when she uses her power

New hair piece is a tangled mass of snakes

Nearly Caught You!

Unfortunately for Medusa (though fortunately for her would-be victims), the hissing of her hair usually gives her hiding place away.

Scales prevent tail-burn when slithering

Tail is hard plastic at the base and flexible at the end

Did You Know?

The long snake tail used to create Medusa's body comes from the LEGO® Ninjago range.

Paintball Player

A rowdy part-time commando

THE PAINTBALL PLAYER constantly challenges his friends to paintball matches, but once the game begins, he starts to shout loudly and crash around. He doesn't realise this makes him an obvious target and he gets splattered with paint right away! No matter how many times he loses though, he remains convinced that he is the best player in town.

Did You Know?

The Paintball Player's new helmet uses the same snap-on visor that comes with the Series 3 Snowboarder.

New paintball gun

Heavy jumpsuit keeps paintballs from stinging

An orange splat on his back means that he was hit by a member of his own team

Worthy Opponent

Win or lose, the Paintball Player loves the thrill of the game. He likes to play against the clumsy Ninja because he is the only one who is worse at dodging paintballs.

Tomahawk Warrior

A uniquely talented ax wielder

EVER SINCE he made it as a youngster, the Tomahawk Warrior hasn't let his tomahawk leave his side. Over the years he has learned how to use it in all kinds of remarkable ways. He can use it to build a boat, open his mail, slice a pizza, and even carve handles for more tomahawks.

Mini Facts

Likes: His tomahawk

Dislikes: Other tools

See Also: Lumberjack (S5)

NICE AX!

Detailed Decoration

The Tomahawk Warrior has one of the most intricate patterns of body printing of any minifigure!

Series 4 Punk Rocker's hair in black

New tomahawk accessory

Feather necklace

Printed loincloth

Did You Know?

The Warrior's tomahawk is the second new ax element created for the LEGO Minifigures line.

ROCKIN' HAIR, MAN!

Mr. Gold

A lucky discovery indeed

SOMEWHERE OUT there is a very special Minifigure called Mr. Gold. Shiny and golden from the top of his hat to the tips of his toes, he never turns up exactly where and when you are looking for him. If you do happen to spot him, it is said that you will be lucky all day long!

Super-classy monocle

Chrome gold finish

Good As Gold

With his dazzling smile, Mr. Gold is the Minifigure everyone wants to meet, especially Conquistador!

Only 5,000 editions of Mr. Gold have been produced

Mini Facts

Likes: Being found by accident

Dislikes: Fingerprints on his spotless finish

See Also: There's no one else like Mr. Gold!

Did You Know?

Mr. Gold was created as an exclusive character to celebrate the 10th series of LEGO Minifigures. He is very rare and the only figure that can't be found in every case of Minifigure bags.

HOORAY, I FOUND MR. GOLD! AND I REALLY AM IN LUCK...BECAUSE LOOK AT WHAT'S ON THE NEXT PAGE!

Toy Soldier

A new Minifigure on the block

NO MATTER where his journey may take him, through city and country, or to distant worlds, the Toy Soldier has a cheery smile and a certainty that he will get wherever he is trying to go. When he finally reaches his destination, he can't wait for the next big adventure to start.

Decorated helmet, or "shako cap" first appeared in LEGO® Pirates sets in 1989

Face and body details replicate classic hand-painted toys

Mini Facts

Likes: Making new friends

Dislikes: Getting lost

See Also: Clockwork Robot (S6)

PARTY

End Of The Quest

The Toy Soldier has traveled through ten amazing series of LEGO Minifigures and met 161 new friends. Now at last he has reached the end of the book. What's going to happen next?

Wind-up key

Special printing on arms and sides of legs

Did You Know?

The Toy Soldier was created exclusively for the *LEGO Minifigures Character Encyclopedia*.

203

WELCOME, TOY SOLDIER!

Index

**LONDON, NEW YORK,
MELBOURNE, MUNICH, AND DELHI**

Editor Pamela Afram
Designer Rhys Thomas
Editorial Assistant Ruth Amos
Additional Designers Liam Drane,
Guy Harvey, Lynne Moulding, Julie Thompson
Senior Pre-Production Producer Jennifer Murray
Senior Producer Lloyd Robertson
Design Manager Nathan Martin
Publishing Manager Julie Ferris
Art Director Ron Stobbart
Publishing Director Simon Beecroft
Additional photography by Gary Ombler

First published in the United States in 2013
by DK Publishing
375 Hudson Street, New York, New York 10014

10 9 8 7 6 5 4 3 2 1
001—187860—Apr/13

A catalog record for this book is available from
the Library of Congress.

ISBN: 978-1-4654-0172-4

Color reproduction by OPUS Multimedia Services Pvt. Ltd.
Printed and bound by Leo Paper Product Ltd, China

ACKNOWLEDGMENTS
Dorling Kindersley would like to thank:
Scarlett O'Hara for proofreading; Daniel Lipkowitz,
Matthew James Ashton, Laurence Dawes,
Chris Bonven Johansen, Ariana Keyser, Elsebeth Søgaard,
Randi Kirsten Sørensen, and Tara Wike at the LEGO Group.

Discover more at
www.dk.com
www.LEGO.com